PALMS OF SOUTH FLORIDA

D1239905

Palms of South Florida

GEORGE B. STEVENSON

University Press of Florida

Gainesville/Tallahassee/Tampa/Boca Raton
Pensacola/Orlando/Miami/Jacksonville

Copyright 1996 by the Board of Regents of the State of Florida
Originally published in 1974 by George B. Stevenson
Printed in the United States of America on acid-free paper
All rights reserved

01 00 99 98 97 96   6 5 4 3 2 1

Library of Congress Cataloging-in-Publication Data

Stevenson, George B.
Palms of South Florida / by George B. Stevenson.
  p. cm.
Originally published: United States: G.B. Stevenson, 1974.
Includes index.
ISBN 0-8130-1441-7 (pbk.: alk. paper)
1. Palms—Florida—Identification. I. Title.
QK495.P17S73 1996
584'.5'09759—dc20   95-49516

The University Press of Florida is the scholarly publishing agency
for the State University System of Florida, comprised of Florida A &
M University, Florida Atlantic University, Florida International Uni-
versity, Florida State University, University of Central Florida, Uni-
versity of Florida, University of North Florida, University of South
Florida, and University of West Florida.

University Press of Florida
15 Northwest 15th Street
Gainesville, FL 32611

CONTENTS

Only one dedication is possible from an author who has been so extremely fortunate as to reside in Fairchild Tropical Garden for four years, and that is . . . .

To the many wonderful people

Whose love and labor have made the Garden

A foretaste of Paradise.

FOREWORD

This is a book for those who are interested in palms, but who have not mastered the highly technical vocabulary used by botanists. The approach herein is not the scientific one, nor is the vocabulary the accepted "botanese" of the professional. Instead of following the customary organization of the material, the author has chosen to present the various species in a system of his own devising, one that emphasizes certain apparent similarities that may be of far more significance to the rank amateur than are the minute floral differences that are of greater importance in determining relationships between the species. Once the reader has become able to identify the common palm species, the more scientific methods can be acquired with less frustration.

The reader is hereby warned that the author of this book has had no formal training in plant science. The information presented in these pages has been derived from three sources. One was the literature. The second was extensive personal observation of the palms in Fairchild Tropical Garden. The third has been the advice, criticism, and suggestions solicited and received from Stanley and Mary Kiem, George Avery, the late Charles (Scott) Donachie, and Don Evans. Without their help, this would have been a much poorer book. The fact that some of their recommendations were not followed frees them from any blame for inaccuracies and misplaced emphasis, without diminishing the author's gratitude. Thanks are also due to Dr. John Popenoe for unrestricted use of the research library and the herbarium of Fairchild Tropical Garden.

The list of species to be included in this book was drawn up by the late Charles (Scott) Donachie, amended by Mrs. Lucita Wait and Stanley Kiem. The goal was the inclusion of those species that are, or have been, offered for sale by the nursery trade or by distribution to members of the Garden.

In selecting the individual palm to be described and sketched, as the representative of the species, I have tried to choose an average tree. In some cases, I was not able to find enough specimens to make a good average, so I made use of what I had available. This means that some, perhaps most, of the data will apply quite well to one individual palm, less well to others of the species in Florida, and even rather poorly to members of the species in other lands. I am consoled by the fact that the specimens in Fairchild Tropical Garden are the parent trees for much of the palm landscaping in Florida, as the species grown here have been disseminated through the Garden's practice of distribution, from the occasional unauthorized appropriation of seeds, and, in some cases, by calculated programs of theft.

Throughout this book, it should be understood that the phrase "in the few individuals known to me" precedes every description of each palm, or of any part of it, and may not apply to other individuals. There should be a large degree of correlation, but I cannot hope that it should be complete. Also, the statistics have been compiled from several sources, and they cannot be expected to cover all individuals within the species under question. A final disclaimer: the opinions on such matters as growth rate, hardiness, and the like are seldom my own but have been taken from people who have had far more experience with palms than I have had.

In the drawings, an attempt is made to depict the general appearance of the entire tree.

Half a leaf of each species is sketched, with care given to the shape and tip area of each segment and leaflet. Where the leafstem possesses armament, it is shown enlarged or natural size. In palmate leaves, the hastula is rendered separately, both above and below, and in that order in the drawing. In pinnate leaves, the tip of the leaflet is given, as is a cross section of the leaflet, to show secondary and marginal ribbing.

The complete flowerstalk is drawn for each species. Where each flower has the organs of both sexes, only one flower is shown; in those cases where male and female flowers occur separately, both are given. In this last case, the male flower will be the one with the pollen-bearing anthers, and the female is usually an acorn-shaped structure with three protruding stigmas.

Flowers and fruit of each species are sketched, though not to scale. Measurement of the fruit is given.

The size of the tree is printed beside the trunk, most often as the height range by the average width. The leaf number, a fairly consistent feature of each species, and an indication of the size of the leaf, also appears. Segments and leaflets have been counted and measured. Leafstem length, where significant, is mentioned. On palmate leaves, the depth of the sinus can be an important identification feature, and the patterning of the sinus stops and the amount of splitting at the tip are also useful. On pinnate leaves, the number of leaflets, the shape of the tip, and the presence or absence of secondary ribbing are indicated.

There is room on South Florida bookshelves for a better book on palms. That thought inspired me to begin this work, and it is still valid. I had planned to combine the relevant data from a few source books, add a few illustrations, and that would be the book. The idea was good but impracticable. Many of the references were incomplete, others contradictory, and some have yet to be written.

Generally speaking, botanical work done a hundred years ago does not meet the more stringent requirements of today's scientists and must be revised by qualified people before the precise identity and relationships of some of the palms can be agreed upon by the botanists. Such a revision, for even one genus, would be a long, expensive process, as it would involve culling all the older references, some in obscure publications in other languages and of limited distribution, and then considerable study of the species in their natural habitats.

The chief problem is in the plants themselves. Each single plant is an individual. We humans try to fit those most alike into pigeonholes, labeled species, genus, and family, but we do not succeed as well as we would like. Nature pays little attention to such artificial categories; her interest is in germ plasma, chromosomes, and their relation to survival. If two individuals can somehow create other individuals, then life goes forward, and man may, if he chooses, try to compartmentalize a free-flowing process, with whatever success he may achieve.

A final word of advice to the reader; learn and use the botanical name of the palm.

Some palms are known by a dozen or more different names in different parts of the world, yet each species has only the one accepted scientific name. Many of the newer palms in our area have no common names in English, nor do they need them, as the botanical name is quite sufficient. However, one need not lose the common touch. A person who refuses to use any term but *Cocos nucifera* for the Coconut Palm, for instance, is probably trying too hard.

Beginners in palm study are often dismayed at the discovery that the botanist does not separate the palms into categories by single characteristics but rather by long lists of criteria. Another discouraging fact is that these factors are described in a jargon that imparts precise meanings to the initiated but that frightens off the casually interested.

Anyone desiring competence in the scientific aspect of palm study must learn a new vocabulary. Among the more exotic (to the layman) terms might be hapazanthic, adaxial, sympodial, caducous, cochleariform, extrorse, prophyllate, funiculus, annulocolpate, and campylotropous, among others.

This book is written in the belief that palms may be discussed intelligently in standard English.

DEFINITIONS

(These definitions suggested in part by Chuck Hubbuch, part by
Professor or Doctor Dransfield)

LEAF: the leafstalk and the blade.

Blade: the portion of the leaf with leaflets or segments.

Leaflet: a division of the blade; usually thin green tissue with one
or more supporting ribs.

Palmate: palm leaf with radiating leaflets or segments.

Pinnate: palm leaf with rows of parallel leaflets or segments.

Costapalmate: palm leaf with some leaflets radiating, others parallel.

Bi-pinnate: palm leaf with leaflets divided again.

Hastula: the enlarged flange at the leafstalk tip where the segments join in a palmate leaf.

Sinus: the space between segments on a palmate leaf.

Sinus stop: tissue mass at the end of the sinus.

Segment: a leaflet, often joined or partially joined to adjacent
leaflets in palmate leaves.

LEAFSTALK: the portion of the leaf that attaches to the trunk and
supports the blade of the leaf.

Unarmed: the leafstalk bare of projections.

Armed: the presence of teeth on leafstalk margins.

Leafspines: modified leaves, hard and sharp, in leaflet row.

TRUNK: the woody portion of the palm; if it is single, it is called
solitary; if more than one form the root mass, it is called multiple.

Ring-scars: marks left on the trunk of some species by the base of
the fallen leaf.

Crownshaft: the tubular, cylindrical column of clasping leafbases at the top of the trunk of some species.

Rootspines: thin, twisted, often branching projections on the
trunks of a few species.

9

BEGINNER'S PAGES

If you live in South Florida, go out and look around you, and take this book along. No matter where you are, you should be able to see several different kinds of palms, and it may well be that you will have as many as eight or ten species within visual range.

Keep in mind that possibly three quarters of all the individual palms in our area belong to about a dozen species, the ones shown on the next two pages. It is recommended that you learn to recognize these, as this knowledge will give you bases for comparison with all the other species.

A word of caution; not all of the trees known as palms deserve the title. The Traveller's Tree, a member of the banana family, is sometimes loosely referred to as the Traveller's Palm. Cycads, chiefly Cycas revoluta and Cycas circinalis, are commonly called Sago Palms. But -- with the cycads, pollen and seeds are produced in dissimilar cones, and each plant bears cones of only one sex.

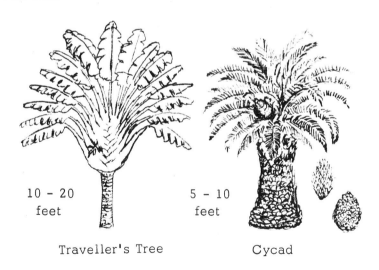

10 - 20
feet

5 - 10
feet

Traveller's Tree   Cycad

COCONUT PALM -- Solitary trunk, clean, no crownshaft; no spines nor teeth on leafstem; pinnate leaflets in one plane, held flat; large fruit.

CABBAGE PALM -- Solitary trunk, clean or covered with leafstem bases, no crownshaft; no teeth on leafstems; costapalmate leaves; long, many branched flowerstalks.

MANILA PALM -- Solitary trunk with crownshaft, clean; no teeth on leafstem; pinnate leaflets in one plane, held in a V; small fruit red. Also known as Christmas Palm.

ROYAL PALM -- Solitary trunk, clean, crownshaft prominent; no teeth on leafstems; pinnate leaflets in several planes; small fruit.

YELLOW BUTTERFLY PALM -- Multiple trunks, clean, with crownshaft; no teeth on leafstem; pinnate leaflets in one plane, held in a V. Wrongly called Areca Palm.

PYGMY DATE PALM -- Solitary trunk with knobby surface, no crownshaft; leafspines on leafstems; pinnate
leaflets in one plane, held flat.

FISHTAIL PALMS -- Solitary or multiple trunks (several
species), no crownshaft; no teeth on leafstems; each
leaflet triangular; suggesting tail of a fish.

CANARY ISLAND DATE PALM -- Solitary trunk with scars
criss-crossing surface, no crownshaft; leafstems with
leafspines; pinnate leaflets in several planes.

QUEEN PALM -- Solitary trunk, clean, no crownshaft;
fiber projections on leafstems; pinnate leaves in many
different planes; small fruit orange.

WASHINGTONIA PALMS -- Solitary trunk, clean or shag
covered, no crownshaft; sharp teeth on leafstems;
palmate leaves; long flowerstalks with few branches.

PRELIMINARY KEY

PALMATE LEAF PALMS
> The segments radiate from a central point,
> as in the palm of the hand.   Page 16

COSTAPALMATE LEAF PALMS
> The leafstem continues on into the blade
> of the leaf and curves downward.   Page 20

FISHTAIL LEAFLET PALMS
> Each leaflet is shaped like the tail of a
> fish (leaf is twice compound).   Page 22

PINNATE LEAF PALMS
> The leaflets are spaced along the midrib
> of the leaf, as in a feather.

PINNATE LEAF PALMS -- INDUPLICATE
> Leaflets folded, margins higher than
> the midrib.   ("In" -- a trough.)   Page 22

PINNATE LEAF PALMS -- REDUPLICATE
> Leaflets folded, midrib higher than
> the margins.   ("R" -- a roof.)

SPINY PALMS
> Spines on leafstem (often elsewhere) Page 22

CROWNSHAFT PALMS
> Leafstem bases clasping   Page 24

NO-SPINE NO-CROWNSHAFT PALMS
> Lacking spines and crowshaft   Page 28

PALMATE   COSTAPALMATE   FISHTAIL

PINNATE

INDUPLICATE   REDUPLICATE

SPINY   CROWNSHAFT   NO SPINES
                                    NO CROWNSHAFT

KEY

PALMATE LEAF PALMS

A. Palmate Leaf Palms with Solitary Trunk

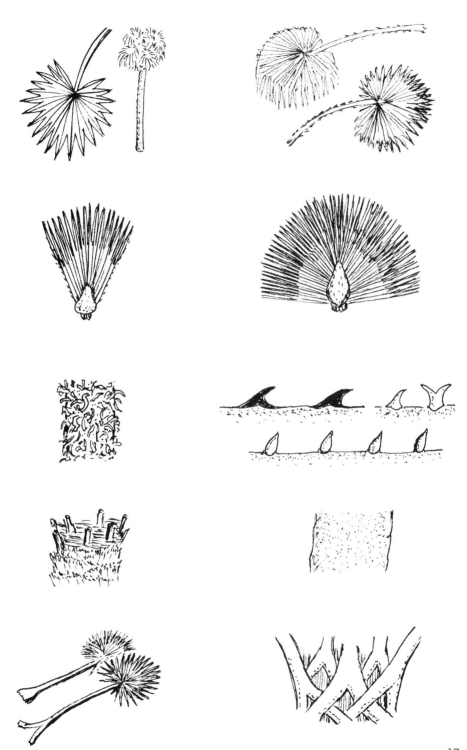

B. Palmate Leaf Palms with Multiple Trunks

C. Palmate Leaf Palms with No Trunk

(NOTE: Seedlings of Nannorrhops ritchiana,
a costapalmate palm, may be palmate; they
are rigid, powdery blue green, and have
no hastula.)

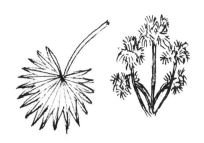

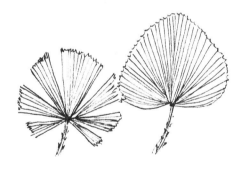

19

COSTAPALMATE LEAF PALMS

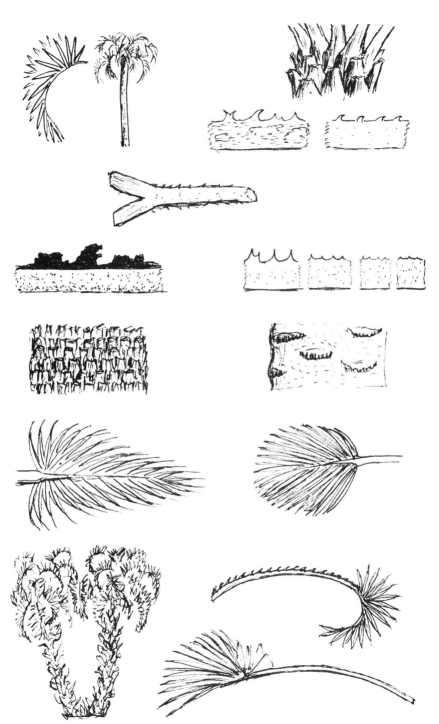

FISHTAIL LEAFLET PALMS

A. Leaflets shaped like fishtails, leaf
   thrice compound

PINNATE LEAF PALMS -- INDUPLICATE

1. Leafspines absent; leaflet margins
   toothed, leaflet tips blunt
1. Leafspines present; leaflet margins
   smooth, leaflet tips pointed

PINNATE LEAF PALMS -- REDUPLICATE
LEAFSTEM WITH SPINES
TRUNK OFTEN SO

A. Spiny Palms with Solitary Trunk
   1. Leaflets in three planes
      2. Leaflets white or gray on underside
      2. Leaflets blue gray on underside, mature
         trunk bulged above middle

   1. Leaflets in one plane
      2. Leaflets joined in groups, tips pointed
      2. Leaflets not joined, tips broad, jagged

B. Spiny Palms with Multiple Trunks

1.

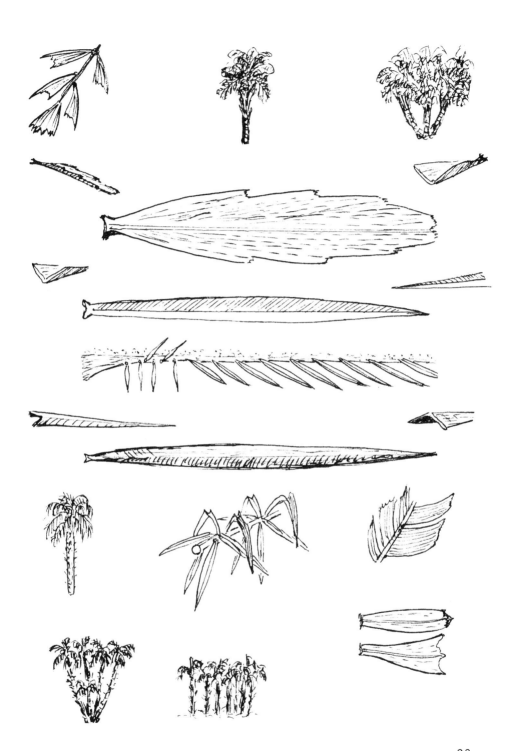

PINNATE LEAF PALMS – REDUPLICATE LEAFLETS
CROWNSHAFT PALMS

A. Crownshaft Palms with Solitary Trunk

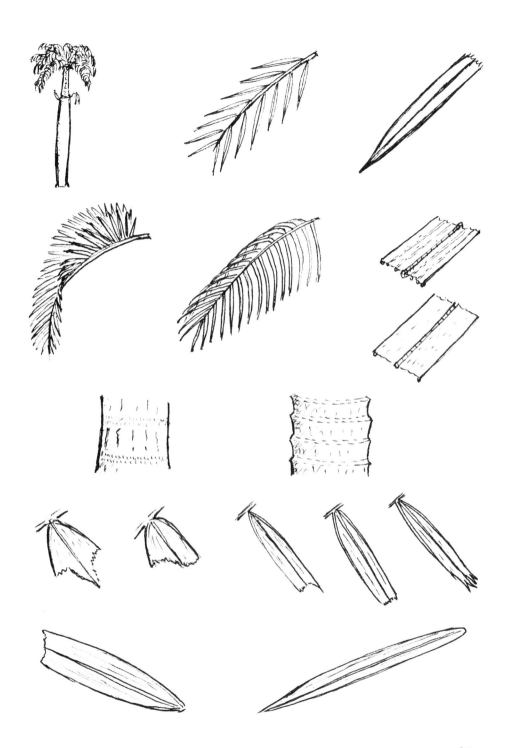

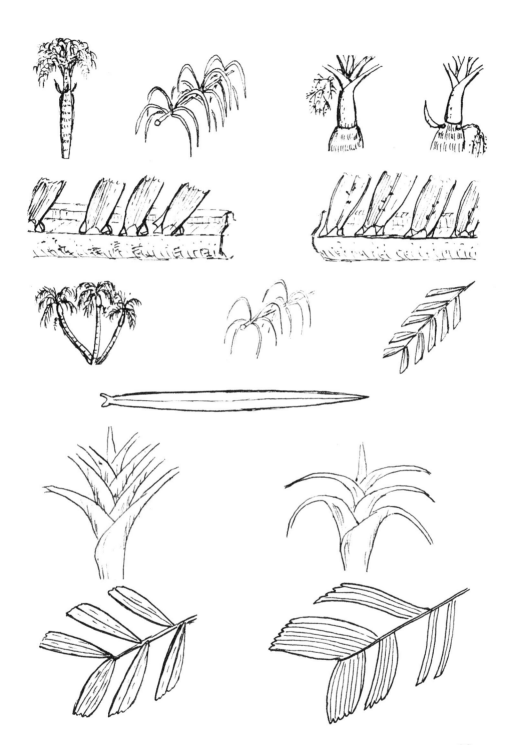

PINNATE PALMS -- REDUPLICATE
NO SPINES -- NO CROWNSHAFT

A. Pinnate, No Spines, No Crownshaft, Solitary Trunk

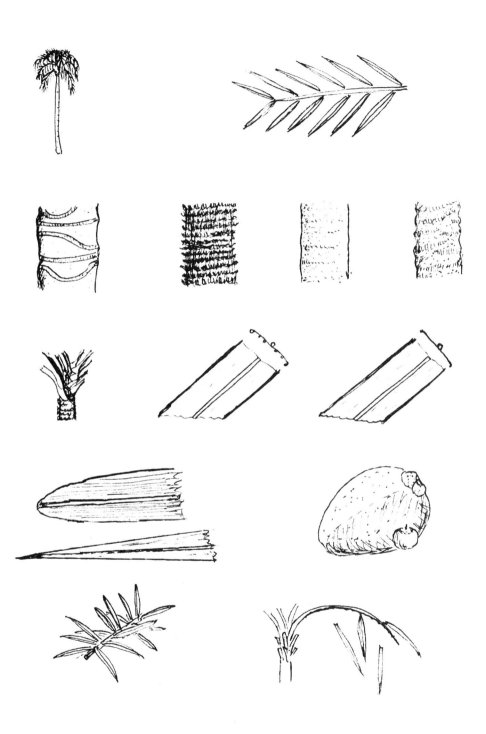

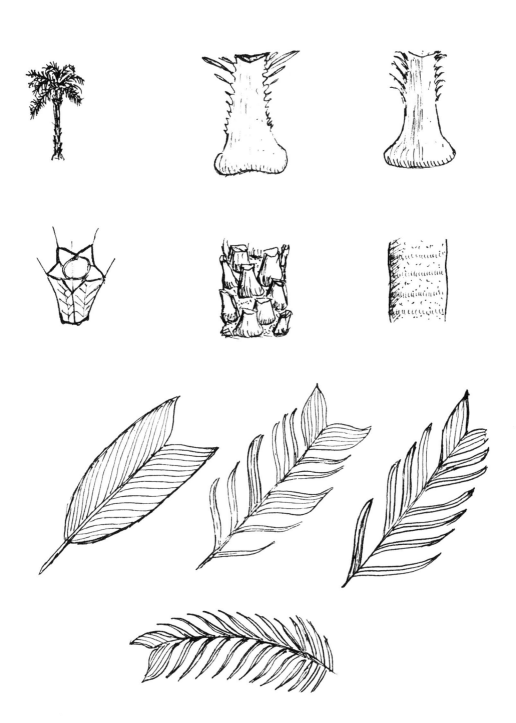

B. Pinnate No-Spine No-Crownshaft Palms with Multiple Trunks

C. Pinnate No-Spine No-Crownshaft Palms with No Trunk

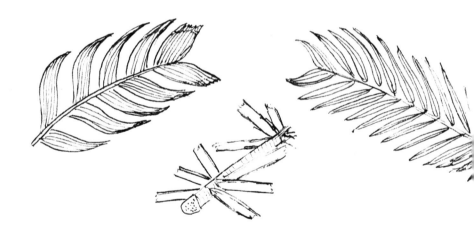

PALMATE LEAF PALMS

WASHINGTONIA

Two species of Washingtonia are known, one from a limited area in California, the other from just over the border in Mexico. Both do well in South Florida, but they hybridize so freely that few local specimens are of pure ancestry. Robusta is the more common with us.

The trunks of Washingtonias may be hidden in a thick shag of dead leaves. Some trees shed this shag, and others may be cleaned by tree trimmers. The surface of the trunk, where exposed, may be partly covered with short fibers and patches of leafstem bases, or it may be clean and slightly scarred.

The leafstem bases are not visibly divided. The margins are armed with sharp teeth, though on mature trees these may be limited to the basal portion. The leaves are large and moderately folded. The leafstem projects into the blade for a few inches. The segments are thin and flexible, drooping at the tip but not dying back as in the Sabals. The segment margins are ribbed. Both species have threads in the sinuses in youth, and both have an extended sinus stop pattern.

Each branch and branchlet of the flowerstalk has a papery bract. The tiny flowers have both sex organs.

WASHINGTONIA ROBUSTA   Mexican Washingtonia
The trunk is taller, narrower, and more tapered, pale gray with no brown, often deeply incised near the base. The narrow segments are more flexible, bending at the sinus stop, and the leaves are a brighter green. Older leaves have few or no threads in the sinuses.

WASHINGTONIA FILIFERA   California Washingtonia
The sturdy trunk is a pale brown. The leaves are not as light a green. They have segments that are stiffer and that bend between the sinus stop and the tip. The threads in the sinuses are conspicuous.

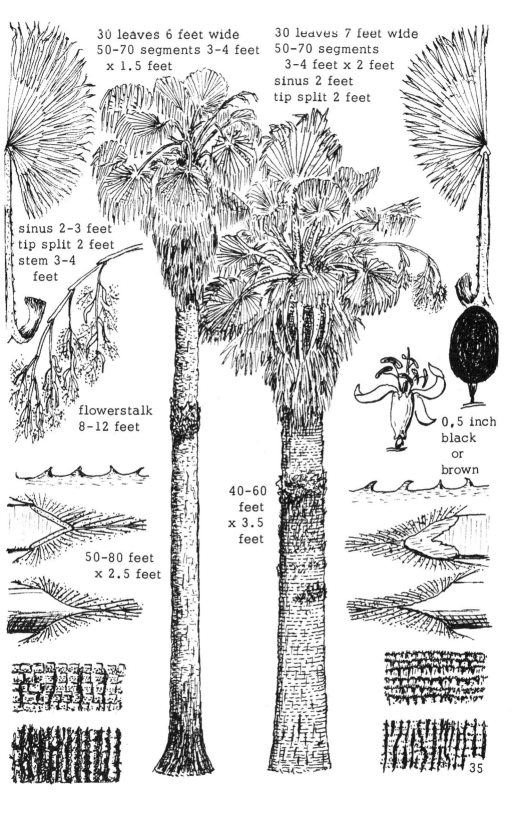

30 leaves 6 feet wide
50-70 segments 3-4 feet
x 1.5 feet

30 leaves 7 feet wide
50-70 segments
3-4 feet x 2 feet
sinus 2 feet
tip split 2 feet

sinus 2-3 feet
tip split 2 feet
stem 3-4
feet

flowerstalk
8-12 feet

0.5 inch
black
or
brown

40-60
feet
x 3.5
feet

50-80 feet
x 2.5 feet

35

COPERNICIA

A wide range of variation of characteristics is found
in the 30 species that make up this genus. One that
they share is a slightly extended sinus stop pattern; a
second is armament on the leafstems of those that have
leafstems, on the leaves of those that are stemless.
As the only other common solitary palms with teeth are
the very tall Washingtonias and the very short Licualas,
this feature is very useful in identification. The only
multiple trunk species has a trunk that is either clean,
or cloaked in spiralled leafstem bases without fiber or
fiber matting, features unusual in multiple trunk palms
with palmate leaves. In all Copernicias, both male
and female sex organs occur in the same flower. All
Copernicias appear to thrive in South Florida.

COPERNICIA RIGIDA   Jata Palm
The trunk, in youth, is covered with fragile, papery
dead leaves; in age, it is clean, and marked with incomplete ring-scars. Leafstems are absent, except
for the 24 inches within the blade of the leaf. Small
sharp teeth arm the outer segments and some segment
midribs. The leaf is exceptionally narrow, enclosing
an arc of about 30 degrees. Segments are stiff and
waxy, split at the apex for about an inch. The hastula
is very large, sometimes reaching 3 feet. Cuba.

COPERNICIA MACROGLOSSA   Cuban Petticoat Palm
A dense cloak of dead leaves hides the trunk until
the old age of the tree, falling to disclose a smooth,
gray, rather slender trunk. Leafstems are absent, and
the segments describe a broad wedge, from about 90
degrees to about 180 degrees, and are not waxy. The
teeth are small but sharp, sprinkled along the margins
of the outer segments and upon the upper side of the
midribs. The rigid segments are split at the apex for
about an inch. The hastula is about 11 inches long.

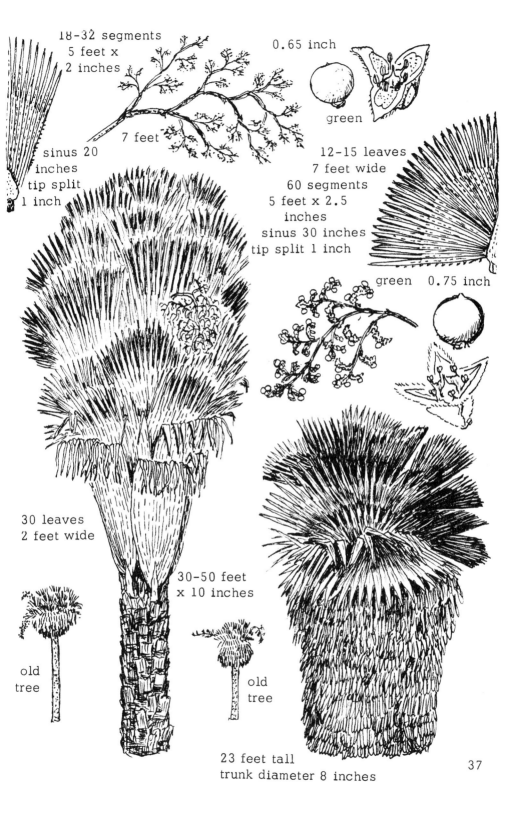

18-32 segments
5 feet x
2 inches

0.65 inch

green

sinus 20
inches
tip split
1 inch

7 feet

12-15 leaves
7 feet wide
60 segments
5 feet x 2.5
inches
sinus 30 inches
tip split 1 inch

green   0.75 inch

30 leaves
2 feet wide

30-50 feet
x 10 inches

old
tree

old
tree

23 feet tall
trunk diameter 8 inches

37

COPERNICIA PRUNIFERA   Carnauba Palm, Wax Palm

The trunk is spiralled with old leafbases in the youth of the tree, the basal portion often remaining in old age. Where this envelope is not found, the trunk is gray and smooth, with incomplete ring-scars visible as slight indentations. The slender leafstems are not divided. Leafstem margins are toothed for the entire length, with large, black, curved hooks. The leaf sinuses are deep, more than halfway to the base. There is no portion of the leafstem within the blade. The segments are waxy and stiff, split at the tip for 1/4 of an inch, and attached to the stem evenly, not at an angle.

This is the famous South American Wax Palm, native to Brazil, and the source of an economically very important industrial wax.

COPERNICIA GLABRESCENS   Guano Palm

The general appearance of this species is similar to that of the Wax Palm, with the following important exceptions. The Guano Palm may, and frequently does, produce suckers from the base of the trunk; the leaf segments are devoid of wax; the trunk is roughened with a few old leafbases and raised ring-scars; the teeth on the leafstems are smaller, lighter, and more numerous; and the tiny flower lacks the hair that coats similar structures in all the other members of the genus. The Guano is a Cuban Palm.

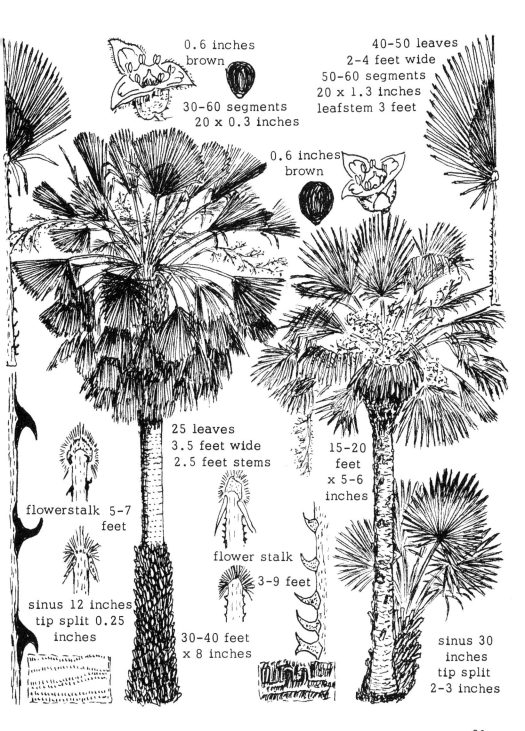

0.6 inches
brown

30-60 segments
20 x 0.3 inches

40-50 leaves
2-4 feet wide
50-60 segments
20 x 1.3 inches
leafstem 3 feet

0.6 inches
brown

25 leaves
3.5 feet wide
2.5 feet stems

15-20
feet
x 5-6
inches

flowerstalk 5-7
feet

flower stalk

3-9 feet

sinus 12 inches
tip split 0.25
inches

30-40 feet
x 8 inches

sinus 30
inches
tip split
2-3 inches

COPERNICIA BAILEYANA   Bailey Copernicia

The surface of the columnar trunk is smooth, gray, and lightly ringed where the tree grows in the open, but has a dark and mottled appearance where the trunk is in the shadows. The leafstems are broad at the base, though not divided, and the margins are very strongly toothed.

The leaves are round in outline, with rigid, waxy segments that are split for 3 to 6 inches from the tip. The portion of the leafstem within the blade is 2 to 5 inches in length.

All of the Copernicias are toothed to a greater or a lesser extent. In those species that possess leafstems, these are very well armed; in those that lack leafstems, teeth are to be found along the margins of the last segments on either side, and sometimes also on the segment midribs.

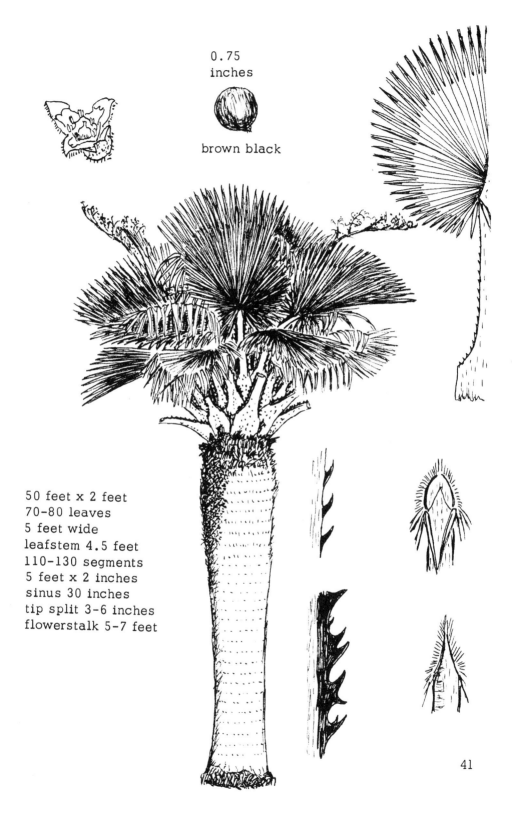

0.75
inches

brown black

50 feet x 2 feet
70-80 leaves
5 feet wide
leafstem 4.5 feet
110-130 segments
5 feet x 2 inches
sinus 30 inches
tip split 3-6 inches
flowerstalk 5-7 feet

41

TRACHYCARPUS

Something like 8 species make up this genus, and it is unfortunate that none of them are suited to our conditions. Seedlings tend to rot at ground level; if they survive, growth is slow. (The smaller plant, opposite, is 3 feet tall after 16 years.) Vigorous specimens may be found from near Jacksonville to Virginia Beach, Virginia. The genus, from Asia, is sparingly represented by T. nana and T. takil in this country, as well as by

TRACHYCARPUS FORTUNEI   Chinese Windmill Palm

The trunk is solitary and straight, and usually rather ragged with remnants of old leafstem bases and a good bit of thin, soft, disorganized brown fiber.

The leafstem bases are not divided, and the stems are exceptionally slender. The margins of these leaf-stems are not really toothed, but have small, rounded bumps, more evident to the touch than to the sight. The leaves are flat, a very dark, dull green above, and nearly silver beneath. The segments are comparatively few in number, and are deeply divided from each other. The sinus stop pattern appears to be completely haphazard. The segments are rigid in young trees; older ones have segments that are more lax, bending near the tip, which is usually split for 1/4 inch. There is a constriction in each segment, between the tip and 1/3 of the length. The small hastula juts abruptly at 45 degrees, and is usually pointed.

The flower stalks are reported to be 1 1/2 feet long, generally with male and female flowers on different trees. The flowers are white to yellow, the fruit blue, bean shaped, and glossy.

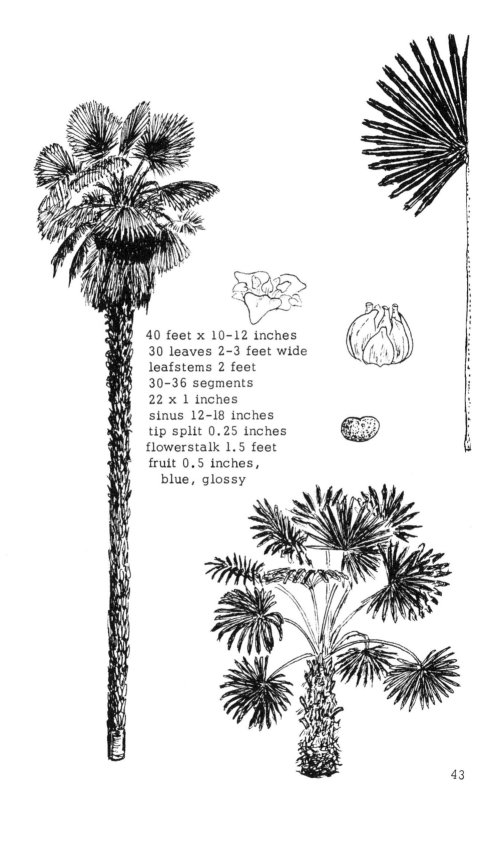

40 feet x 10-12 inches
30 leaves 2-3 feet wide
leafstems 2 feet
30-36 segments
22 x 1 inches
sinus 12-18 inches
tip split 0.25 inches
flowerstalk 1.5 feet
fruit 0.5 inches,
   blue, glossy

THRINAX

About 12 species of Thrinax palms are known, from the shores and islands of the Caribbean Sea. All are highly recommended for South Florida, for their complete adaptation to soil and weather, their resistance to disease, and their good appearance.

Thrinax palms have trunks that are solitary, slender, sometimes slightly curving, their surfaces smoothly irregular. They are clean in old individuals, but shaggy in young ones, and there is a considerable amount of disorganized fiber at the base of the leafstems. When clean, the trunks are gray to brown gray, with incomplete ring-scars noticeable but not prominent. Old trees often have a large root mass at the base.

The unarmed leafstems split at the base, an important feature in separating members of this genus from those of Coccothrinax. The leaves are glossy above, medium green to yellow green, and dull beneath, even silvery in some species. The leaves are usually lax and deeply folded. The segments are ribbed on the margins, these becoming thick dividing ribs between the segments. In some species, the segments are split at the tips, in others they are entire. The sinus stop pattern is oval.

The flower stalks appear among the leaves, and may extend well beyond them. The simple, papery bracts are numerous -- sometimes as many as 24 -- and the branches divide again into branchlets. The fruit is white, with the rind soft and spongy. Each flower has both male and female parts, with 6 stamens.

THRINAX MICROCARPA   Silvery, Brittle Thatch
The under side of the leaf has a silvery cast. The smallest segments are pulled up and forward. The tip of the hastula is rounded. The fruit is stemless. Common on some of the Florida keys. "Peaberry Palm."

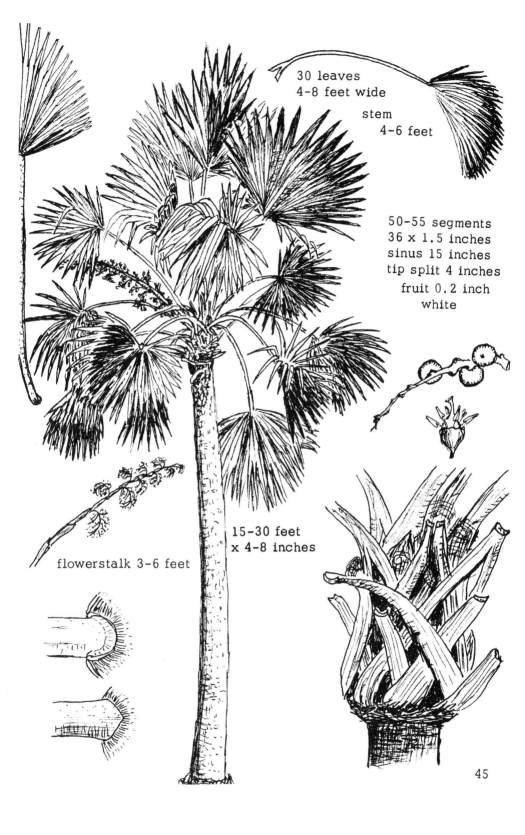

30 leaves
4-8 feet wide

stem
4-6 feet

50-55 segments
36 x 1.5 inches
sinus 15 inches
tip split 4 inches
fruit 0.2 inch
white

15-30 feet
x 4-8 inches

flowerstalk 3-6 feet

45

THRINAX FLORIDANA   Florida Thatch Palm

This is the other native thatch palm. Its leaves are
dull green on the under side. The leafstem is usually
shorter, and the hastula more pointed, than are those
of the other species. The fruit has a short stem. As
with T. microcarpa, this species is spread throughout
the Caribbean Basin, and at least one variety is recognized. This is T. floridana var. jamaicensis. It is
slightly larger in all respects.

THRINAX EXCELSA   Jamaican Thatch Palm

This species is probably quite rare in South Florida,
with most of the palms called by this name being, in
reality, the above mentioned variety of T. floridana.
Excelsa has larger leaves, perhaps a third larger than
those of the large variety of Floridana, with the leaf
segments being about twice as wide. The under side
of the leaf is a yellow green.

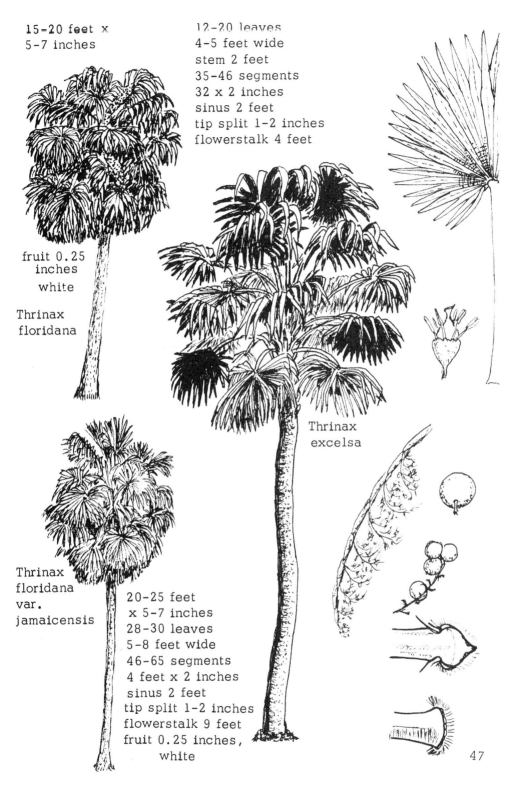

15-20 feet x
5-7 inches

12-20 leaves
4-5 feet wide
stem 2 feet
35-46 segments
32 x 2 inches
sinus 2 feet
tip split 1-2 inches
flowerstalk 4 feet

fruit 0.25
inches
white

Thrinax
floridana

Thrinax
excelsa

Thrinax
floridana
var.
jamaicensis

20-25 feet
x 5-7 inches
28-30 leaves
5-8 feet wide
46-65 segments
4 feet x 2 inches
sinus 2 feet
tip split 1-2 inches
flowerstalk 9 feet
fruit 0.25 inches,
white

47

COCCOTHRINAX

One of the 50 or more species of Coccothrinax is native to the Florida keys, Cape Sable, and a few places in the Everglades: the others are scattered around the shores of the Caribbean. These are palms of limestone soils, perfectly adapted to South Florida, at their best in partially shaded situations.

They are solitary palms, small to medium in height and in girth. The trunks are smooth and a light gray in most species, with a shag of fiber mats and dead leafstem bases in others, and completely covered in straw colored masses of loose fibers in one species.

The leafstem bases are not divided, and leafstems are not armed. The leaves are a glossy dark green above, lighter green, silvery, or gray below, usually
(continued on page 50)

COCCOTHRINAX ARGENTATA   Florida Silver Palm
Of the species of this genus considered in this account, this one has the deepest silver on the underside of the leaves, the thinnest and most lax segments, and the deepest sinuses. Growth rates for individuals vary with the location. On Big Pine Key it takes about five years for this palm to develope a trunk eight feet tall; several, in the Miami area, have reached that height after 40 to 50 years. The palm is hard to transplant.

COCCOTHRINAX ARGENTEA   Hispaniolan Silver Palm
This species is slightly larger in all respects than the previous one, the leaf segments being about twice as wide. The leaves are duller, have less silver on the under side, and are more rigid. The leaves are flat and the leaflets are folded; in the above species, the reverse is true.

16 leaves 3 feet wide
stems 2.5 feet
43 segments
2 feet x 1 inch
sinus 18 inches
tip split
2-3 inches
flowerstalk
2 feet
fruit 0.5 inch
black

18 leaves
3 feet wide
stem 3 feet

3-20 feet
x 6 inches

48 segments
2 feet x 2 inches
sinus 14 inches
tip split
1.5 inches

flowerstalk
1.5 feet

0.3 inches
black

49

COCCOTHRINAX   (continued)

flat or with the central segments elevated slightly. The
segments have thin marginal ribs, and are split at the
tip. The sinus stop pattern is oval.

The flower stalks are generally shorter than the leafstems. The stalk subdivides into branches and then
into branchlets. The flowers have male and female sex
organs, and are small and white. The fruit is purple to
black, thin-skinned and juicy. The stamen number is 9.

COCCOTHRINAX DUSSIANA
Leafstems are longer and leaves are wider in this
species than in the two preceding. Each segment has
a crease, a fold halfway between rib and margin. The
underside of the leaves has very little of the silvery
color that distinguishes the first two species. Trunks
may be smooth and gray, or wrapped in well-organized
fiber matting and studded with dead leafbases. This
is the fastest growing Coccothrinax in common use.

COCCOTHRINAX CRINITA   Old Man Palm
The most immediately evident feature of C. crinita
is the mass of straw colored fiber that bulks twice as
large or more as the trunk. The leaves, shining and
dark above, are dull gray beneath, and on very long
stems. The flower stalk is much longer than those of
the other species. The Old Man Palm is from Cuba.

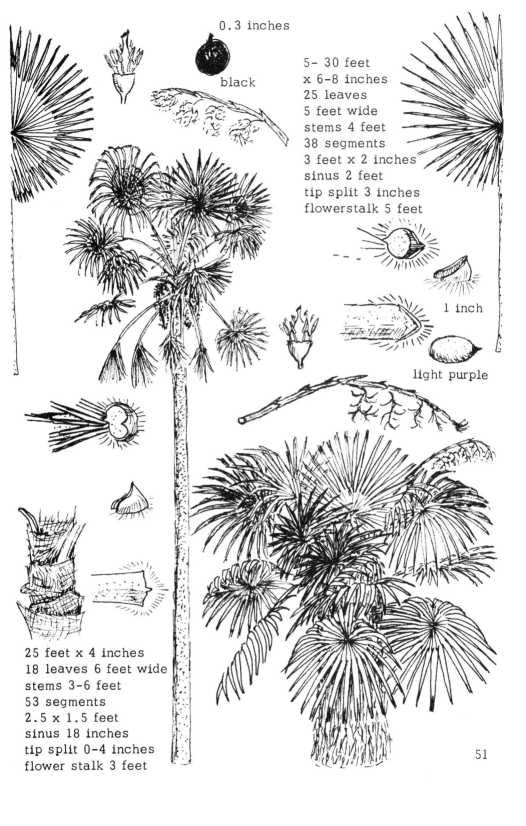

0.3 inches

black

5- 30 feet
x 6-8 inches
25 leaves
5 feet wide
stems 4 feet
38 segments
3 feet x 2 inches
sinus 2 feet
tip split 3 inches
flowerstalk 5 feet

1 inch

light purple

25 feet x 4 inches
18 leaves 6 feet wide
stems 3-6 feet
53 segments
2.5 x 1.5 feet
sinus 18 inches
tip split 0-4 inches
flower stalk 3 feet

51

COCCOTHRINAX MIRAGUAMA

Apparently quite a variable species, C. miraguama has been described as tall and slender or as short and thick, with fruit either black or red. The leaves of the seedlings are about 24 inches across, with 25 segments of a dark, dull green above, silvery or mottled beneath, the tips abruptly pointed. Partly grown trees may have wider leaves -- to 5 feet in diameter -- with trunks that are smooth with barely perceptible ring-scars, or hidden in fiber matting and old leafstem bases. Mature trees sometimes have small leaves.

The plane of the leafstem and the plane of the blade of the leaf are at an angle to each other, from 45 degrees to almost 90 degrees. The leaflets are curved in cross section, rather than folded. The fiber wrapping of the trunk, where present, is close and neat.

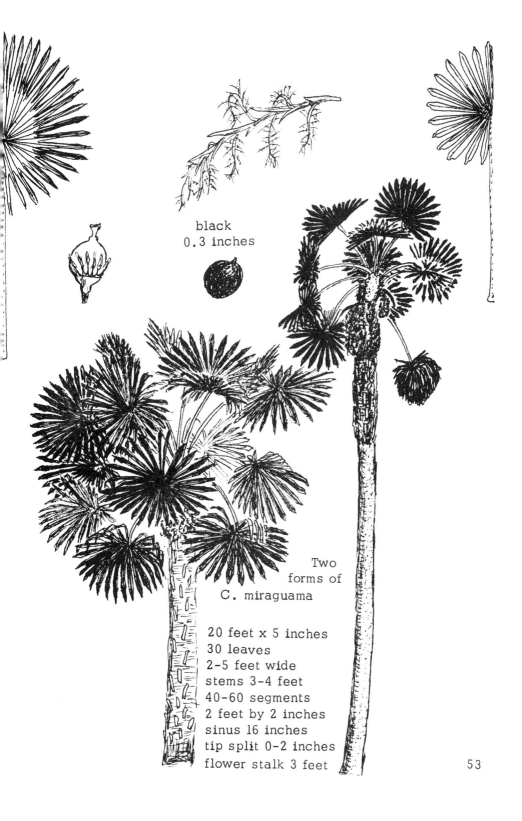

black
0.3 inches

Two
forms of
C. miraguama

20 feet x 5 inches
30 leaves
2-5 feet wide
stems 3-4 feet
40-60 segments
2 feet by 2 inches
sinus 16 inches
tip split 0-2 inches
flower stalk 3 feet

53

CRYOSOPHILA

The genus is Central American, from Mexico through Panama, and has nine species. Both those mentioned herein do well in South Florida, perhaps at their best in partial shade and rocky limestone soil. Neither is common at this time.

The trunks of the Rootspine Palms are solitary and straight, and are distinguished by their covering of aerial roots; these are light gray, brittle, often twisted, sometimes branched, but never sharpened into spines. The trunk itself is a very light gray. Brown fiber and a white pulp cover the part of the trunk in the crown of leaves.

The leafstems are long, unarmed, and divided at the base. Leaves are very dark above, very light beneath. The arrangement of the sinus stops appears to be random. The leaf segments are lax, without marginal ribs, but with 3 to 5 interior ribs on the underside, and with tips that are thick and sharply pointed. Each segment has several pleats, or creases, from base to tip. The segments are composed of a rather fragile tissue that frequently tears, separating some of the segments all the way to the base.

The flowers are crowded together in a solid mass, each having both sex organs. There are 6 or more bracts on the stalk, none on the branches.

CRYOSOPHILA WARSCEWICZII   Rootspine Palm
The rootspines tend to be longer and more numerous in this species than in the one below. The leaves are dull above, and barely silvery beneath. The hastula is prominent and pointed.

CRYOSOPHILA ARGENTEA   Silvery Rootspine Palm
The leaves are glossy green above and quite silvery beneath. The hastula is low and rounded.

1 inch
brown

1 inch
brown

20-45 feet
x 5 inches
30 leaves
6 feet wide
stems 6 feet
45 segments
3.75 feet
x 2 inches
flower stalk
2.5 feet

20-45 feet
x 4-5 inches
30 leaves
7 feet wide
stems 4-6 feet
45 segments
3 feet x
x 2 inches
flower stalk
3 feet

sinuses irregular
tips not split

55

SCHIPPIA

Schippia concolor is one of the relative newcomers
to South Florida, and one of great promise. It is an
understory tree in its native habitat, the forests of
Central America, but it seems to do well in the open
sunlight, with no special protection against normal
weather eccentricities. It is the only species in its
genus, as far as is known at this time.

SCHIPPIA CONCOLOR

The slender trunk is solitary, gray, and somewhat
roughened, marked with vertical fissures. Very young
trees have the trunk swathed in fiber, but older plants
have clean trunks except just below the crown, where
old leafbases break down into soft, spongy tissue.

The leafstems are long, thin, unarmed, concave, and
deeply divided at the base. Leaves are a dark, glossy
green above, dull beneath. Each leaf is folded, with
the basal leaflets at 90 degrees to the plane of the
leafstem. The segments are sharp pointed, usually not
divided at the tip. The hastula is a ring, with a point
in the center. The sinus stop pattern is extended.

The flower stalk has several major stems, each one
dividing several times, and each major division has its
own bract. Each flower has both male and female sex
organs. The fruit is much larger than that of any of the
Thrinax or Coccothrinax species with which this plant
might be confused.

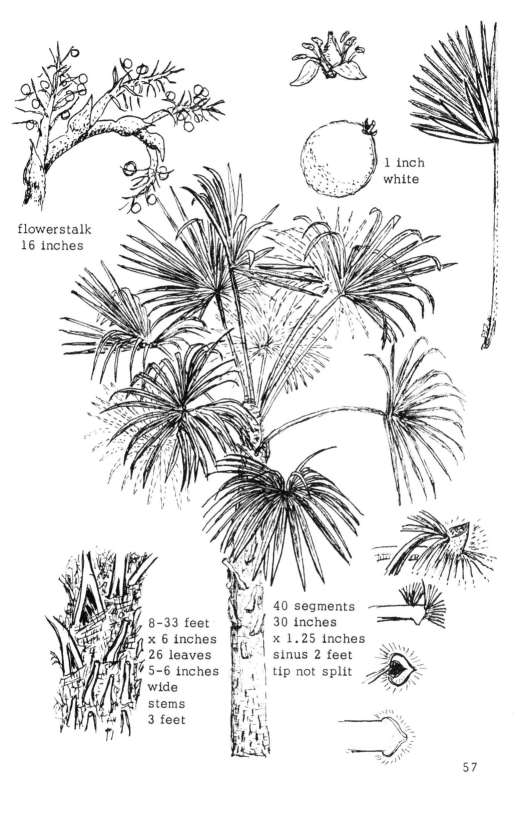

flowerstalk
16 inches

1 inch
white

8-33 feet
x 6 inches
26 leaves
5-6 inches
wide
stems
3 feet

40 segments
30 inches
x 1.25 inches
sinus 2 feet
tip not split

57

LICUALA

Licualas are small palms, slow in growing, shade loving understory plants from the East Indies. Some 100 species have been described, and perhaps a dozen of these have been introduced in South Florida. One, which may be the only one with undivided leaflets, is becoming fairly common, and is easily identified.

LICUALA GRANDIS
The trunk is solitary, short, slender, and dark, with incomplete ring-scars projecting as sharp ridges that are broken by vertical fissures. A few leafbases near the crown may persist, their margins breaking down into small amounts of brown fiber.

The leafstems are not divided; they are studded with sharp, hooked teeth, at least near the trunk. The leaf is truly costapalmate, but this is apparent only upon close inspection. The narrow segments are undivided.

The flower stalk is as long as the leaves, with about a dozen bracts, and every major branch has its own bract, as well. Every flower has both sex organs.

The specific names of lauterbachii, peltata, rumphii, paludosa, and spinosa, among others, are given to the other licualas that may be encountered rarely in South Florida. All differ from L. grandis in having divided leaves, usually with a number of segments in groups, and a number of them are said to have multiple trunks. Distinguishing between these very similar species is extremely difficult, and the descriptions of them in the botanical literature seldom fit the plants as we know them. It is wiser to await a revision of the genus than to attempt to puzzle out the identities of these confusing plants.

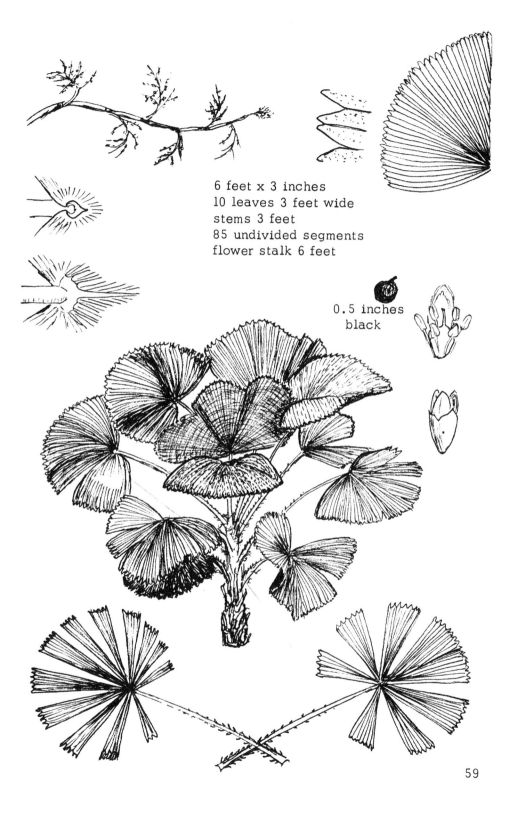

6 feet x 3 inches
10 leaves 3 feet wide
stems 3 feet
85 undivided segments
flower stalk 6 feet

0.5 inches
black

ACOELORRHAPHE

The one species in this genus is a native of brackish swamps of South Florida, the West Indies, and parts of Central America. It does not require a wet situation, and will thrive in good soil in upland sites. When it is planted in limestone soils it may become chlorotic, the leaves turning yellow. The remedy is to feed it on manganese, magnesium, and iron. A healthy specimen is a most attractive palm, and the species is another of our natives that can be highly recommended.

ACOELORRHAPHE WRIGHTII   Everglade, Paurotis Palm

The many trunks touch one another at the base, thus causing the outer ones to lean away from center. Each trunk is completely covered with well organized fiber matting and long, thin leafstem bases.

The leafstems have undivided bases, and are armed with sharp orange teeth at intervals of about one inch. The leaves are a medium to a light green, and lighter, almost silvery, beneath. The segments are divided half way to the base, and the margins are not ribbed. The tips are split from 4 to 8 inches. The sinus stop pattern is exaggeratedly extended.

The flower stalk is rather short, and is erect until it is pulled down by the weight of the fruit. There are 3 papery, tubular bracts. Both sex organs are found in each flower.

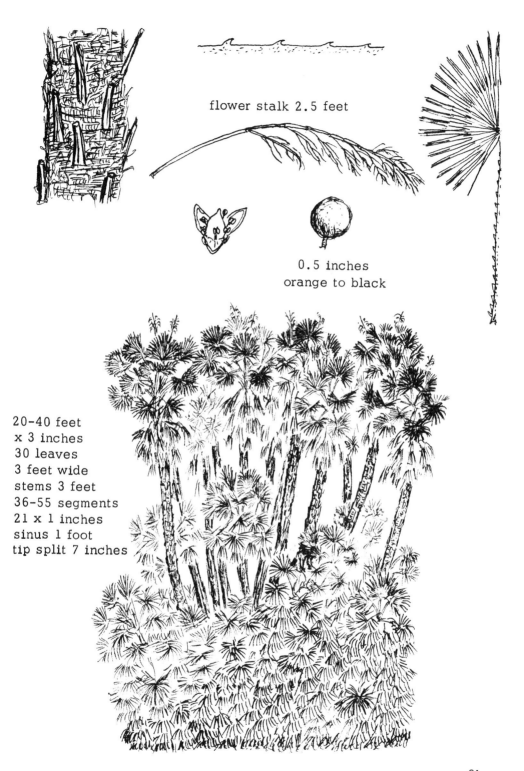

flower stalk 2.5 feet

0.5 inches
orange to black

20-40 feet
x 3 inches
30 leaves
3 feet wide
stems 3 feet
36-55 segments
21 x 1 inches
sinus 1 foot
tip split 7 inches

ZOMBIA

Haiti, on the island of Hispaniola, is the home of the one species in this genus. It is a very attractive palm, well suited to South Florida, although still not well known here. It is at its best in full sun.

ZOMBIA ANTILLARUM   Zombie Palm

The multiple trunks grow in close proximity, often touching one another. Each is enveloped in a matting of fibers, resembling an inflexible burlap, with a row of extended sharp pointed strands that turn downward.

The unarmed leafstems are very thin, less than half an inch wide. The leaves are a bright green above, silvery beneath, and are flat to slightly folded. The segments are moderately lax, slightly ribbed, split at the tip for 1/4 inch. The sinus stop pattern is irregular. On the upper surface of the leaf, the hastula has three points, the outer ones rounded, the center one sharp-and drawn out. On the underside of the leaf, a single sharp point marks the center of a small, triangular hastula.

The flower stalk is short, and twice branched; there are about 12 bracts, one at each branch. The fruit is white and spongy. Both sexes occur in each flower.

A smaller variety is recognized, var. gonsalezii. The leaves are about 18 inches across. The species may be trunkless.

The Zombie Palm will hybridize with some of the Coccothrinax species, and the offspring show more of the parentage of the latter, but produce multiple trunks.

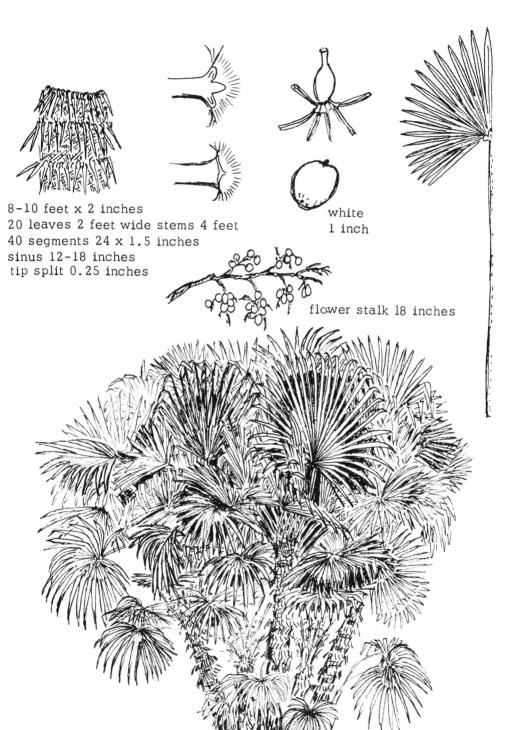

8-10 feet x 2 inches
20 leaves 2 feet wide stems 4 feet
40 segments 24 x 1.5 inches
sinus 12-18 inches
 tip split 0.25 inches

white
1 inch

flower stalk 18 inches

63

CHAMAEROPS

Europe's only palm is one of the two in this genus, which also occurs in northern Africa. The species in common use has several forms, varying from one another in height, color of leaves, length of leafstems, and color and size of the fruit. It is not harmed nor even set back by cold weather, and it may be that our region is too warm for it. We find it to be very slow growing, and it seldom sets viable seeds here. It is susceptible to both Ganoderma and the ambrosia beetle.

CHAMAEROPS HUMILIS   European Fan Palm

In nature, the trunks sucker at the base, producing multiple stems; some owners prune the suckers, thus creating a solitary trunked palm. Most specimens attain a height of 4 to 6 feet, but it is not unusual for an individual to reach 20 feet. The trunks are widest near the crown. A shag of dead leaves may cover the trunk, beneath which plates of fibers may be found; or, the leaves may fall, leaving an occasional leaf-stem base as a flat projection; or, the trunk may be clean, with a multitude of thin, ridged ring-scars crowding upon one another.

. The leafstem bases are broad and flat in life, but decay to disclose an inner core of woody tissue that decreases in size between trunk and leafstem. The stems are armed, and are concave, with bases that are undivided. The leaves may be dark green, gray blue, or silvery, and either glossy or dull. Stiff, sharply pointed segments are divided to half or more of the segment length, and are deeply split, the half segments being very narrow. The sinus stop pattern is extended.

The flower stalks are short, clustered at the top of the tree, each with one pointed-tipped bract that opens along the side. Most trees bear flowers of only one sex, but a proportion -- some authorities say 1 in 30 -- have flowers containing both sexes.

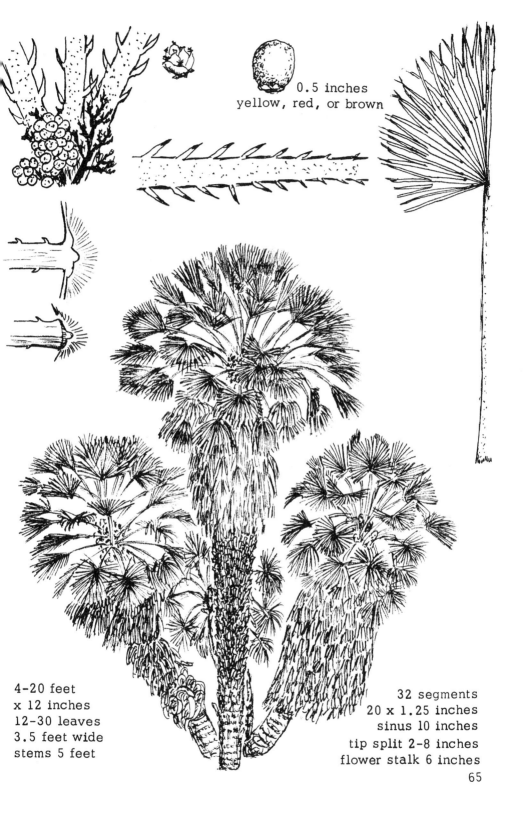

0.5 inches
yellow, red, or brown

4-20 feet
x 12 inches
12-30 leaves
3.5 feet wide
stems 5 feet

32 segments
20 x 1.25 inches
sinus 10 inches
tip split 2-8 inches
flower stalk 6 inches

65

SERENOA

The southeastern United States, along the coast
from South Carolina westward to Louisiana, is the
natural range of the one species in this genus. It is
our only native branching palm. Its natural adaptation
should make it a prize ornamental, but it is extremely
hard to transplant, and the seedlings grow slowly.

SERENOA REPENS   Saw Palmetto
The trunks are sprawling, with fat, twisted roots
pushing outward wherever the trunks crawl along the
ground. An occasional branch may cant upward at a
lazy angle for 20 feet, but most are under 6 feet tall.
Old leafbases, closely crowded together, surround the
trunks; they persist, reddish, irregular plates amid a
small amount of brown fiber matting.

The leafstem margins are rough near the leaf, the
small bumps swelling to become teeth near the base.
The leaves are slightly folded, twisted, and vary from
yellow green to a cloudy blue green to a silver white.
The segments are stiff, without marginal ribs, and are
split from the tip, from an inch to as much as a foot.
Small, fragile hastulas occur on both sides of the leaf,
and the leafstem extends into the blade for less than
an inch. The sinus stop pattern is extended. There
are three silvery-leaved varieties that can be found
in the scrub in the Fort Lauderdale and West Palm
Beach area, east of the Intracoastal Waterway.

The flower stalk is as long as the leaves, each with
two tubular bracts as the base of the stalk and one for
each of the 6 to 8 branches. The branches divide into
branchlets. The small white flowers contain the organs
of both sexes.

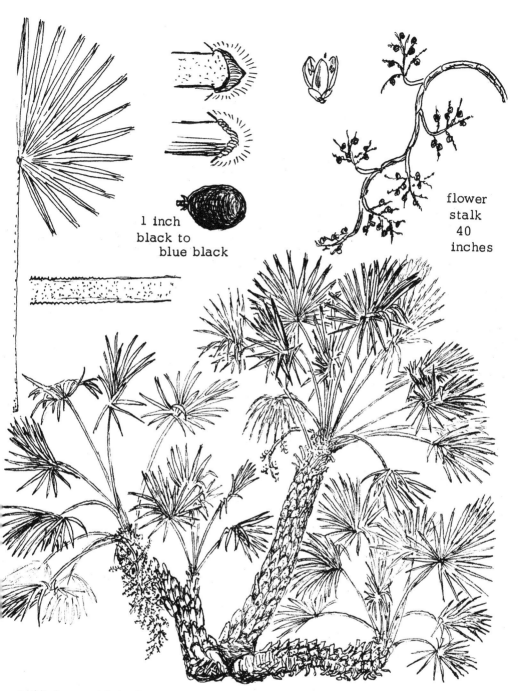

1 inch
black to
blue black

flower
stalk
40
inches

4-20 feet x 18 inches
12-30 leaves 3.5 feet wide, stems 5 feet

32 segments 20 x 1.25 inches
sinus 10 inches, tip split 2-8 inches

67

RHAPIS

Southeast Asia is the homeland of about 9 species of
Rhapis Palms. One is now very well established in the
gardens and nurseries of South Florida, and another is
sometimes available, though not common. They are
propagated by division, as they seldom produce seeds,
and somehow this has made them very variable in number of leaf segments, color, and height, although the
qualities that make for variety often disappear when
the plants are grown in deep shade. They prefer shaded
sites and good soil, but can withstand the effect of full
sunlight. A single plant can generate a thicket.

RHAPIS EXCELSA   Lady Palm

The thin trunks are covered with persistent leafbases
and dark fiber matting. On older stems, the trunk is
clean, ringed like bamboo, black with tan ring-scars.
The intensity of the green color of the upper side of the
leaf is variable, but the undersides are always paler.
All other palmate palms have the sinus stops at the top
of the induplicate fold; only in Rhapis are the sinus
stops at a lower level than the leaf tissues. This is
due to an extra folding of the segment, a feature that
may be unique to this genus. The sinuses are deep,
almost to the small, pointed hastula.

The flower stalks are short, with 2 or 3 bracts. The
male and female flowers are on different stems.

RHAPIS HUMILIS   Lady Palm

Generally shorter than the above species (note that
it is reported that this situation is reversed in California), this species has a better defined fiber matting
at the leafbases, a thinner trunk, smaller leaves, narrower segment tips, and deeper sinuses. It is usually
found as a house plant.

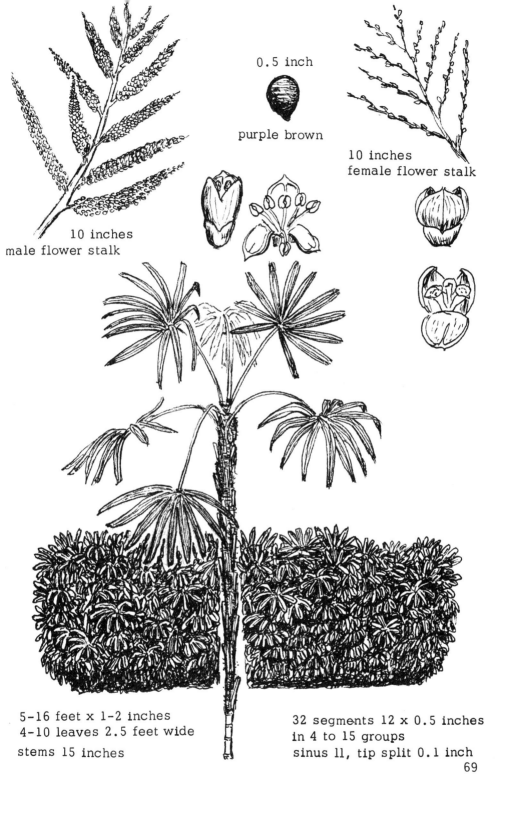

0.5 inch

purple brown

10 inches
female flower stalk

10 inches
male flower stalk

5-16 feet x 1-2 inches
4-10 leaves 2.5 feet wide
stems 15 inches

32 segments 12 x 0.5 inches
in 4 to 15 groups
sinus 11, tip split 0.1 inch

69

RHAPIDOPHYLLUM

This genus has but the one species. It is found in Florida, Georgia, the Carolinas, and Mississippi, but it is not common anywhere in its range. It is used to a colder climate than ours, but does very well here in deep shade, and can be hardened gradually to full sunlight. It is slow growing.

RHAPIDOPHYLLUM HYSTRIX   Needle Palm
There is no trunk, but rather a short crown made up of old leafbases and new leaves, that may reach 5 feet but is usually less than a foot high.

The thin leafstems are neither armed nor divided, but the copious fiber matting at the leafstem base produces thin, sharp, black needles that point upward, and may be from 4 to 12 inches long. The flat leaves are dark green above and silvery green below. The sinuses and the sinus stops are not at the marginal ribs of the segments, but to one side, in effect causing one segment to be wider than another. The segments are stiff, with 3 or 4 points to each tip.

The flower stalk is short, hidden among the spines and the leaves. The flowers are very small, purple in color, with the male flowers on one plant and the females on another.

3-5 feet high, no trunk
6-18 leaves 4 feet wide
leafstems 2 feet
15-20 segments
18 x 0.75 inches
sinus 17 inches
tip split 0.25 inches
flower stalk 12 inches
fruit 1 inch, purple brown,
    wooly

COSTAPALMATE LEAF PALMS

BRAHEA

The 17 Braheas are Mexican palms, from the parched
west coast of that country, and they have been less
than successful in South Florida. Southern California
grows them well; here, those in good, rich soil seem
to be ill adjusted, often short lived, but better results
may be had with those planted in marl fill. All of the
Braheas are susceptible to attacks of the palm weevil.

BRAHEA ARMATA   Big Blue Hesper Palm
The trunk is solitary, with a slightly swollen base,
and rough with leafbase remnants and incomplete ring-
scars. The crown contains a large amount of fiber.

The base of the leafstem is not divided. Leafstems
are armed with large, dark thorns, and a wooly wax
covers the under side. The ice-blue leaves are very
thick and stiff, strongly folded, and the leafstem extends more than halfway through the blade. Segments
are attached to the leafstem on a slant. Though split
at the tip, they do not droop. The sinus stop pattern
is indented.

The flower stalk is longer than the leaves. Male and
female organs occur in each flower.

At least three other species of Brahea are cultivated
in California, and may also be here. B. elegans is a
small palm, less than 10 feet tall, resembling B. armata
in color. B. edulis grows to a height of 30 feet, has a
smooth trunk, thin leafstems that can be thornless, and
leaves that are light green on both sides. B. brandegeei
reaches 100 feet, with old leafstem bases patterning the
trunk, leafstems with heavy armament and yellow edges,
and leaves that are dull green above, whitish beneath.
Until very recently, the genus was known as Erythea.

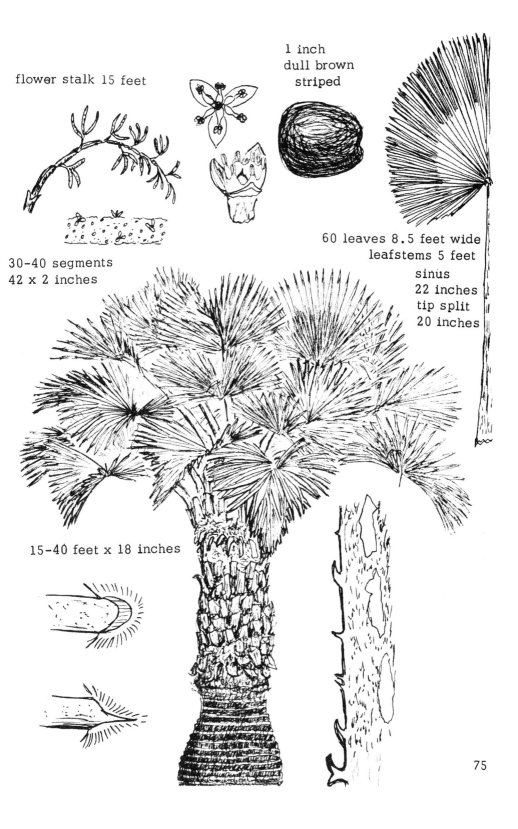

flower stalk 15 feet

1 inch
dull brown
striped

30-40 segments
42 x 2 inches

60 leaves 8.5 feet wide
leafstems 5 feet
sinus
22 inches
tip split
20 inches

15-40 feet x 18 inches

75

LIVISTONA

Livistonas, with 30 species from Australia and the Asian mainland, seem to be well adapted here. Some are fairly common, and of increasing popularity.

The solitary trunks are variable in appearance with the species; within the species, they may also vary with age. All have a large quantity of fiber in the crown. Young trees have a long-waisted look, as the region from which the leafstems issue may stretch for 6 to 10 feet, where in most palms it is a foot or less.

The leafstem base is not divided. The leafstems are armed with sharply pointed teeth, especially numerous toward the base. The leaves are folded, with a short section of the stem within the blade. The segments are split at the tip. The sinus stop pattern is extended.

The flower stalk is long and slender, with both male and female parts in the same flower.

LIVISTONA CHINENSIS   Chinese Fan Palm

This is the most common palm of the genus in South Florida. The trunk is brown at first, with crowded, incomplete ring-scars that wear away to a gray, smooth exterior. Spines usually occur on the lower half of the leafstem, but not always. The leaves are folded, and are a dull olive green. Segment tips are lax, a prominent feature of the species.

LIVISTONA ROTUNDIFOLIA

Taller and faster growing than the above, this palm has a trunk that is more likely to be partly covered with leafbases and fiber in youth. As these fall, the complete ring-scars appear as red brown lunes broken by vertical fissures. The leaves are a darker green, with minute, interrupted yellow lines. The segments are stiff, and do not droop. Sinuses are less than half the segment length.

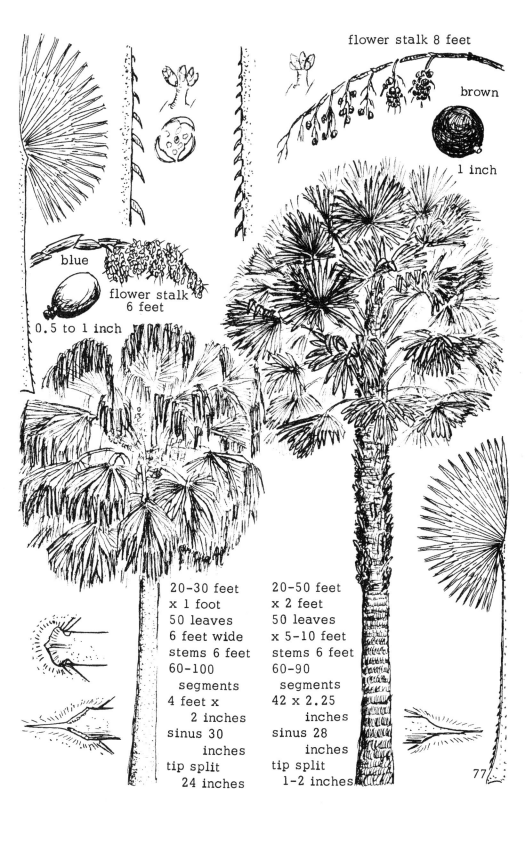

flower stalk 8 feet

brown

1 inch

blue

flower stalk
6 feet

0.5 to 1 inch

20-30 feet
x 1 foot
50 leaves
6 feet wide
stems 6 feet
60-100
    segments
4 feet x
    2 inches
sinus 30
    inches
tip split
    24 inches

20-50 feet
x 2 feet
50 leaves
x 5-10 feet
stems 6 feet
60-90
    segments
42 x 2.25
    inches
sinus 28
    inches
tip split
    1-2 inches

77

LIVISTONA   (continued)

LIVISTONA AUSTRALIS   Australian Cabbage Palm

The brown trunk of this species is rough; the incomplete ring-scars forming sharp-edged, crowded ridges once the leafbases and fiber slough off. The segments are moderately wide, drooping, with tips split to about a foot. The sinus is half the length of the segments. This palm is slow growing.

LIVISTONA DECIPIENS

Of the four species, this one has the thinnest leaf segments, the deepest sinuses, and the largest sinus stops. The ring-scars are complete, shiny red brown plates at the point of attachment to the warm brown trunk. The leaf segments attach obliquely, and are sharply folded, flattening and becoming quite lax at the halfway mark. The tips are deeply split, really forked. This species is fast growing, but the leaves tend to become frayed by the wind.

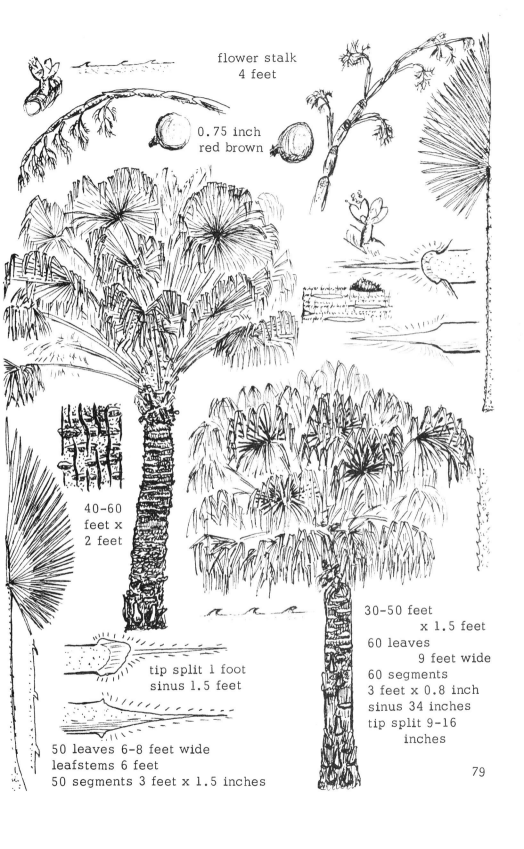

flower stalk
4 feet

0.75 inch
red brown

40-60
feet x
2 feet

tip split 1 foot
sinus 1.5 feet

50 leaves 6-8 feet wide
leafstems 6 feet
50 segments 3 feet x 1.5 inches

30-50 feet
x 1.5 feet
60 leaves
9 feet wide
60 segments
3 feet x 0.8 inch
sinus 34 inches
tip split 9-16
inches

79

BORASSUS

The Palmyra Palm shares with the Coconut the honor
of being among the most useful of trees to mankind.
In its Indian homeland, it is the source of edible oil,
of lumber, sugar, wine, and many other valuable pro-
ducts. There are 6 or 7 other species of Borassus, of
little economic value, from Africa eastward through New
Guinea, little known outside their native lands.

BORASSUS FLABELLIFER   Palmyra Palm

The trunk is straight, tall, and sturdy; in youth it is
completely covered with divided leafbases; in age it
may be clear, or nearly so. The ring-scars are complete, with tufts of fiber at the two points of attachment of each leafstem. Most trees are swollen at the
base, and some have a swelling above the midpoint.
Young trees are "long-waisted," the crown stretched.

The leafbases are divided. The leafstems have a
row of sharp edged plates, irregular in outline and
jet black in color, on each margin; on old leafbases,
these become gray but remain sharp. No wool, down,
nor wax occurs on the leafstems. The leaves are a
gray green, and moderately folded. Leaflets are very
stiff, the margins slightly ribbed, the tips split.

Male and female flowers are borne on different trees.
The male flowers are small and numerous, sunken in
pits in foot-long banana shaped structures. The fruit
is nearly round, with 3 seeds in a sweet smelling husk
of yellow fiber. Male trees have larger leaves.

The South Florida climate agrees with the Palmyra
Palm, but its size restricts its use to the larger garden
or public park. Among its peculiarities is the way in
which the seedling developes; it grows straight downward for about three feet, then makes a complete turn
and grows upward and out into the sunlight.

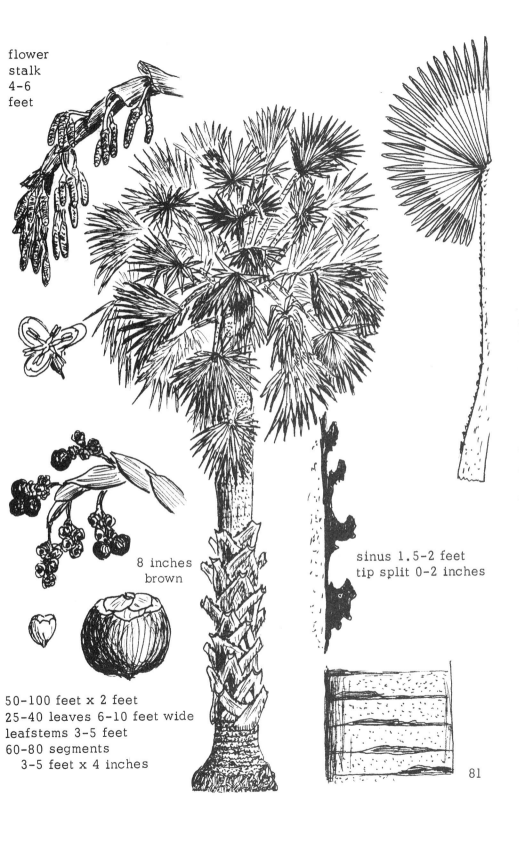

flower
stalk
4-6
feet

8 inches
brown

sinus 1.5-2 feet
tip split 0-2 inches

50-100 feet x 2 feet
25-40 leaves 6-10 feet wide
leafstems 3-5 feet
60-80 segments
    3-5 feet x 4 inches

81

CORYPHA

Of the 8 species of Corypha, from tropical Asia, two have been brought to South Florida. They are seldom encountered here, as few gardens have room for such giants. Record leaves have measured 16 feet across, the widest in the palm family.

The gigantic, solitary trunks are covered with gray leafstem bases in youth, but are clean or partially so in age. The ring-scars are complete. There is no fiber in the crown.

The leafstem bases are divided, and persist after the body of the leaf has broken away. The margins of the leafstems are toothed. The leafstem itself is very heavy and extends more than half way into the deeply folded leaf. The segments are stiff and strongly ribbed, with blunt tips that are usually split.

Coryphas mature in 30 to 80 years, devoting all their energies in youth to vegetative growth. Upon reaching maturity, each tree sends up a flower stalk from the top of the crown to a height of 20 feet. Cream white flowers (60 million, in one count) with both sex organs form on the numerous branches. After the year it takes the fruit to form and ripen, the tree dies.

CORYPHA UMBRACULIFERA   Talipot Palm
This is the largest species, but has the smallest of teeth on the bright green leafstem. The trunk does not have the spirals that distinguish the following species.

CORYPHA ELATA   Buri Palm
The trunk is marked by spiralled swellings. Segments of the leaves are narrower and more brittle than in the above species, and leafstem teeth are larger.

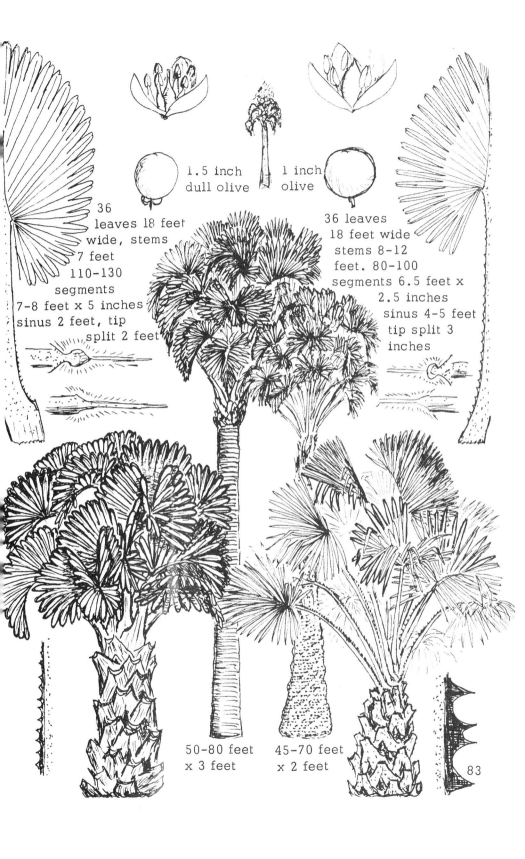

1.5 inch
dull olive

1 inch
olive

36 leaves 18 feet wide, stems 7 feet 110-130 segments 7-8 feet x 5 inches sinus 2 feet, tip split 2 feet

36 leaves 18 feet wide stems 8-12 feet. 80-100 segments 6.5 feet x 2.5 inches sinus 4-5 feet tip split 3 inches

50-80 feet x 3 feet

45-70 feet x 2 feet

ere is only one species in this genus from Mada-
car. The palm is well suited to local conditions,
and would be more widespread in South Florida were it
more obtainable.

BISMARCKIA NOBILIS   Bismarck Palm
The trunk is solitary, straight, and wide, dark gray,
rather rough, with shallow vertical fissures and with
incomplete ring-scars. Younger trees have the trunk
covered with old leafbases; older trees have a clean
trunk. Where the ends of the leafbases break away
from the trunk, they leave a shiny brown plate.

The leafstems divide at the base. They are long,
heavy, blue green to light gray, and are covered with
a wooly wax on the underside. The leafstem margins
are armed with small, sharp teeth. The segments are
rigid and a distinctive light gray green. New growth
is downy. The segments are heavily ribbed on the margins, with tips that are pointed but soon splitting.
The hastula is small, a lop-sided spoon.

Male and female flowers occur on different trees.
Each flower stalk has several bracts at the base, and
one for each of the 8 to 10 branches. Each branch is
swollen larger than its stem, with the small flowers
sunken in pits.

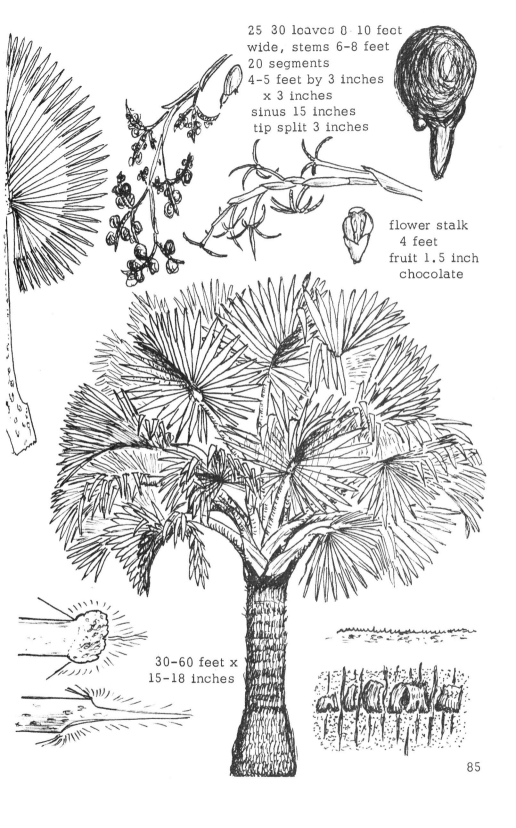

25 30 leaves 8 10 feet
wide, stems 6-8 feet
20 segments
4-5 feet by 3 inches
  x 3 inches
sinus 15 inches
tip split 3 inches

flower stalk
4 feet
fruit 1.5 inch
chocolate

30-60 feet x
15-18 inches

85

LATANIA

The three species of Latania Palms are native to the Mascarene Islands, in the Indian Ocean. All three are now fairly common in South Florida, and all are subject to the attacks of the palm beetle.

Latania trunks have swollen bases, and are clean of old leafstems. They are solitary and straight, with no fiber in the crown. The ring-scars are complete.

The leafstems are divided at the base, and are armed with sharp teeth that wear away as the leafstem ages. Quantities of gray wax and wooly down form on the underside of the leafstems. The large leaves are deeply folded, a dull gray green. The leaflets are stiff, with minutely toothed margins and unsplit tips. Leafstems project half way through the blade of the leaves.

Male and female flowers are on different trees, with the males set in pits in the swollen branches. There are 3 seeds in each fruit, differently shaped in each of the species. Cross-breeding is possible, but rare.

LATANIA LONTAROIDES   Red Latan Palm
Midribs and leafstems are streaked with red on new leaves. The gray trunk has wide, bulging ring-scars. The hastula is pointed and elevated.

LATANIA LODDIGESII   Blue Latan Palm
Midribs and leafstems are mottled with blue. The brown gray trunk has narrow, undulating, ridged ring-scars, and slight bulges where the old leafstems had been attached. The hastula is pointed and flat.

LATANIA VERSCHAFFELTII   Yellow Latan Palm
Midribs and stems are yellow. The brown trunk is rough with low ridged horizontal ring-scars, seldom bulging. The hastula is blunt and flat.

flower stalks
3-6 feet

32 segments
4-5 feet x 3 inches
sinus 26 inches
tip not split

8-24 leaves
4-8 feet wide

20-50 feet x
10 inches

2 inches

yellow green

L. lon.

L. lod.   L. ver.

L. lon.   L. lod.   L. ver.

87

SABAL

There are about 25 species of Sabal, from North and South America. Four of these are native to some part of the United States. The Sabal palmetto is the state tree of Florida. Sabals flourish in South Florida.

The trunk is solitary, and two species are trunkless. A shag of dead leaves is sometimes found, but this is an individual pecularity. All Sabals have lots of fiber.

The leafstems are deeply divided and unarmed. The typical leaf has a stout, deeply curved stem that penetrates completely through the blade. The segments are stiff and divided deeply, the last ones bent downward. The leafstem traces out to a sinus stop; in all the other costapalmate genera, to a segment midrib. The sinus stop pattern is extended.

The flower stalk is long, slender, and has numerous bracts and branches. Flowers and fruits are small. Sex organs of both male and female are in each flower.

SABAL PALMETTO   Cabbage Palm
The trunk is brown and rough, with incomplete ring-scars on young trees; smooth and gray on older ones. Old leafbases persist on some trees, not on others. Long, thin fibers are plentiful at the base of the leaf-stems. The leaves are dull medium green on both sides with yellow blotches on the older ones. The segment tips are split for about 2 feet back from the very long, thin point, and the segments are stiff except near the tips. The flower stalk is as long as the leaves.

SABAL MEXICANA   Rio Grande Palmetto
This species is nearly indistinguishable from the one above. It is supposed to be slightly shorter, with less fiber in the crown, more likely to be covered with old leafstem bases. The flower stalk is shorter than the leaves, and the fruit is brown, not black. The tree is from the Rio Grande Valley, and is rare in Florida.

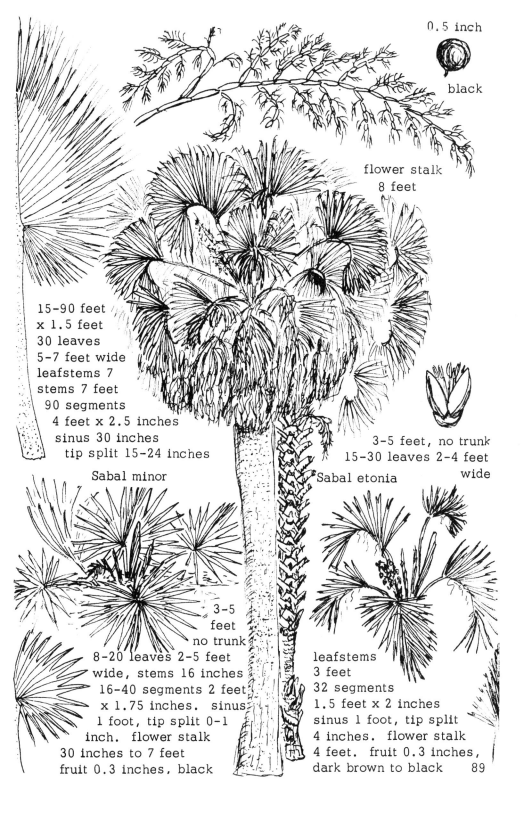

0.5 inch

black

flower stalk
8 feet

15-90 feet
x 1.5 feet
30 leaves
5-7 feet wide
leafstems 7
stems 7 feet
90 segments
4 feet x 2.5 inches
sinus 30 inches
tip split 15-24 inches

3-5 feet, no trunk
15-30 leaves 2-4 feet
wide

Sabal minor

Sabal etonia

3-5
feet
no trunk
8-20 leaves 2-5 feet
wide, stems 16 inches
16-40 segments 2 feet
x 1.75 inches. sinus
1 foot, tip split 0-1
inch. flower stalk
30 inches to 7 feet
fruit 0.3 inches, black

leafstems
3 feet
32 segments
1.5 feet x 2 inches
sinus 1 foot, tip split
4 inches. flower stalk
4 feet. fruit 0.3 inches,
dark brown to black   89

SABAL   (continued)

SABAL MINOR   Dwarf, or Blue, Palmetto
   A trunkless species, with a straight or curved underground stem of varying length. Rare individuals will
make a trunk to 7 or 8 feet. The leafstem within the
blade is very short, but extends completely through to
the sinus stop, at times dividing the leaf in two lobes.
Leaves are flat, or slightly folded, light blue gray or
gray green. Segments are thick and rigid, not split at
the tip, and often arched upward. Native to Florida,
the palm ranges from North Carolina to Texas.

SABAL ETONIA   Scrub, or Corkscrew, Palmetto
   Another species with no visible trunk, this one has a
spiralled underground stem. The leaves are half as big
as those of Sabal minor, and are on shorter leafstems.
They are deeply folded, stiff, and green, with threads
in each sinus. The fruit is larger. The range of this
species is from Lake to Broward County, Florida.

SABAL CAUSIARUM,   Puerto Rican Hat Palm
   The lower portion of the massive, imposing trunk is a
smooth, light gray, with a few projections; the upper
part is brown, ringed, and with tufts of fiber. The leafstems are sturdy, stiff, and unarmed. The leaves are a
gray green with yellow blotches, strongly folded. Segments are stiff, usually split 1 1/2 feet from the tip,
dying back but unbending. The flower stalk is longer
than the leaves. Native to Puerto Rico.

SABAL MAURITIIFORMIS
   The light brown trunk usually displays complete ring-
scars on the clean lower portion, with a network of old
leafbases below the crown. The leaves are less hooked
than those of S. palmetto, and are glossy above, dull
beneath. The segments are paired, each pair split to
within 6 inches of the base, and are lax, with tips that
are shorter and wider than those of S. palmetto. Native
to Central and South America.

30-50 feet x 2 feet
40 leaves 1 foot wide
stems 4-6 feet
80 segments
    4 feet x 2 inches
sinus 20 inches
tip not split
flowerstalk 8 feet

40-80 feet x 9 inches
26 leaves 1 foot wide

24 segments 3 feet
    x 1.5 inch
sinus 4 feet
tip split 1-18 inches
flowerstalk 12 feet

fruit 0.3-0.5 inch

fruit 1.5 inch

91

HYPHAENE

The genus has about 30 members, from Africa, Arabia, and India. They are similar in all of the apparent features, differing largely in fruit and flower structure, and are treated collectively in this book. A few individuals of at least 5 species have been grown here, but the growth rate is too slow and young plants have too seldom been obtainable for the palms to become popular. All Hyphaenes prefer near desert conditions.

HYPHAENE spp.   Doum, Gingerbread Palm

Hyphaenes are most noted for their branching habit, an extremely rare trait among palms. The main trunk may be solitary, but more often several to 4 trunks or more originate from the parent plant. Young trees have the trunk covered with white to gray leafbases; older ones are at least partially clean. The surface is almost black, divided into rectangles by the thin, rather deep vertical fissures; these fissures are light brown, as are the complete ring-scars. The points of attachment of the leafstems are often marked by fiber tufts.

The leafstems are armed with large, sharp, hooked teeth, black in youth but gray with age. Hyphaenes do not produce wax nor down on the leafstems. The leaves are a gray green and very deeply folded, the terminal segments rotated through 100 degrees. The segments are stiff, with ribbed margins and with tips that are sharp pointed but often split.

Male and female flowers occur on different trees. The male flowers are yellow. The fruit is dull orange on the common species, but can range from yellow through black, and the shape is also variable. One common name comes from the color of the fruit; it is barely edible, a famine food. Five species known to be in South Florida are H. thebaica, H. turbinata, H. schatan, H. indica, and H. coriacea.

15-40 feet x 1 foot
20-30 leaves
    4 feet wide
stems 3 feet
20 segments 3 feet
    x 2 inches
sinus 22 inches

tip split 0-1 inch
flower stalk 4 feet
fruit 3 x 2 inches,
brown , black, or yellow

93

NANNORRHOPS

In their native home in Afghanistan and Pakistan, the four species of Nannorrhops must withstand a wide temperature range, from hot, dry summers to winters with a moderate snowfall and biting winds. The one species that is at all common in South Florida is very cold hardy, and should be more widespread. The slow rate of growth, and it is among the slowest of palms, may account for its comparative scarcity with us.

NANNORRHOPS RITCHIANA   Mazari Palm

The several trunks are prostrate for the first several feet, then they turn upward. A mature stem fruits and dies back part way, but not before a replacement stem grows from just below the crown, so that the tree is temporarily branched. Each trunk is thick, the large, thin plates of old leafstem remnants forming a cover.

The leafbases are divided and unarmed, though some references mention tiny teeth. On most mature trees, quantities of bright orange wool are produced by the bases of the leafstems. The light green leaves have a deeply curved profile, the leafstem projecting through the blade. There is no hastula. The segments divide deeply from one another, and are split down the center for half their length. The sinus stop pattern is indented. (Young plants have stiff leaves of a white green, powdery, and are palmate rather than costapalmate.)

The flower stalk is a massive structure at the top of the trunk, towering 6 feet above the leaves, with many 5 foot branches, each subdivided several times. The flowers contain organs of both sexes.

5-25 feet x 15 inches
40 leaves 4 feet wide
stems 40 inches
30 segments 4 feet x 1.5 inch
        sinus 3 feet
        tip split 15 inches
        flowerstalk 40 inches
        fruit 0.5 inch, orange brown

PRITCHARDIA

The islands of the Pacific Ocean are home to about 35 species of Pirtchardia. Hawaii has 26 of the total, while Fiji and Samoa have the two that have been introduced so successfully here.

These are solitary palms of moderate height, with a smooth, erect trunk. A moderate amount of fiber forms within the crown.

The leafbases are not divided, and leafstem margins are not armed. The leafstems are short, thick, bright green, and usually coated with a straw colored wax. The leaves are slightly folded, with the leafstems extending about half way through the blade. Leaves of younger trees are often larger than those of older ones. The stiff segments point from ahead to about 90 degrees to each side. The sinus stop pattern is extended.

The flower stalk has one set of branches, crowded at the end. Each fruit has a swollen, globular stem. The flowers have both sex organs in the same blossom.

PRITCHARDIA PACIFICA   Fiji Island Fan Palm
This is the taller of the two, with the thicker trunk, less likely to have a swollen base. The flower stalk is shorter, about as long as the leafstem. The fruit is twice the size of that of the Thurston Palm.

PRITCHARDIA THURSTONII   Thurston Palm
The trunk is usually more brown, and has more vertical fissures than the above. The flower stalk hangs down well below the leaf. There are wooly scales on the underside of the leaf near the leafstem.

Another Pritchardia, P. affinis, the Kona Palm, may occur here, but rarely. The leaves are folded, sinuses are deeper, and the fruit several times larger.

8-30 feet x 1 foot
36 leaves 4-8
   feet wide
stems 31 inches
55-90 segments
3 feet x 2 inches
sinus 12 inches
tip split 2 inches
flowerstalk 1 foot
fruit 0.5 inches,
blue black

10-30 feet
  x 8 inches
25 leaves 4-8
   feet wide
stems 3 feet
56 segments
3 feet x 2 inches
sinus 1 foot
tip split 2 inches
flowerstalk 6-10
    feet

fruit 0.25 inch
red to black

97

FISHTAIL LEAFLET PALMS

CARYOTA

These are the Fishtail Palms, unlike any other palm genus in that the leaves are twice compound. The odd name refers to the shape of the leaflet.

Twelve or more species of Caryota are native to the Asian mainland, Indonesia, and the Philippines. The genus is incompletely known, which means the names now in use may be replaced by others when the genus is revised. With the scanty evidence now available, it is not possible to classify some of the species. In our area, it is the custom to name any cluster fishtail Caryota mitis, any tall, solitary one Caryota urens, and to use the name Caryota cumingii for any short, solitary individual.

The trunks, solitary or multiple, are covered with long, pointed leafstem bases and black fiber matting; where these have worn away, the trunks are green to gray, beneath a layer of whitish wax, and are marked with dark ring-scars set well apart.

Leafstem bases clasp the trunk at the point of their attachment, but are split down the back so that there is no cylindrical sheath. There are about 12 secondary stems, with 12 leaflets or so to each one. The leaflets have several veins on the underside.

The flower stalk is short and thick, with many thin, long branches. The flowers are crowded thickly, one central female and two males.

CARYOTA MITIS   Clumping Fishtail Palm
The many trunks are distinctive for the species in this area. The tree is long lived, as new shoots grow constantly to replace those that have died.

6 or more stems 8-10 leaves leaflets 4-7 inches
12-40 feet tall 4-9 feet long flowerstalk 1-2 feet
4-8 inches wide stems 2-4 feet fruit 0.5 inch, black

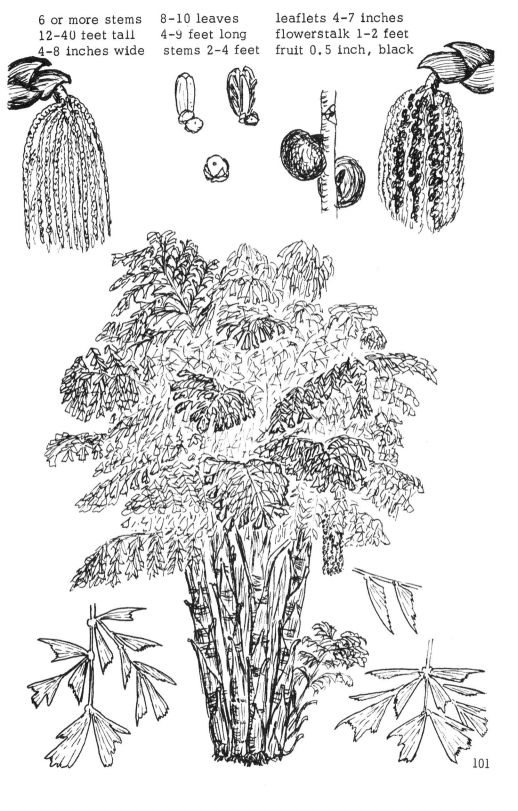

CARYOTA   (continued)

In Caryota, Arenga, and Wallichia, the tree does not flower until it reaches maturity. Then the first flower stalk appears at the top of the plant, the successive ones at each lower node (ring-scar). When the lowest of these has ripened its fruit, the tree is dead, if it is a solitary species, or that one trunk dies, if it is one of the multiple trunked individuals.

The name Caryota urens was given by Carl Linnaeus to the first fragmentary sample of a fishtail palm known to science. Since then (1753) it has become apparent that there are a dozen or so distinct species of fishtail palms, but no one can be sure which was the one that Linnaeus named. He had only a portion of a leaf, and the modern scientist needs leaf, flower, and fruit in order to classify the species. This work has not been done, so that a degree of confusion exists.

Of the various solitary species of fishtail palms, it is currently accepted to restrict the name Caryota urens to India, Caryota aequatorialis to Malaya, Caryota ochlandra to China, and Caryota cumingii to the Philippine Islands. Caryota rumphiana ranges from Java through the Phillipines to New Guinea and New Caledonia. The features that have been used to separate the species are not always clear, and the books are not always in accord. Several solitary fishtails have been brought to South Florida, under accepted and unaccepted names, and it appears that the confusion will be with us until the genus is revised in the light of modern knowledge.

CARYOTA URENS   Fishtail Palm
The solitary trunk differentiates this palm from C. mitis, and larger size from C. cumingii.

CARYOTA CUMINGII   Fishtail Palm
This is the short fishtail with the single trunk.

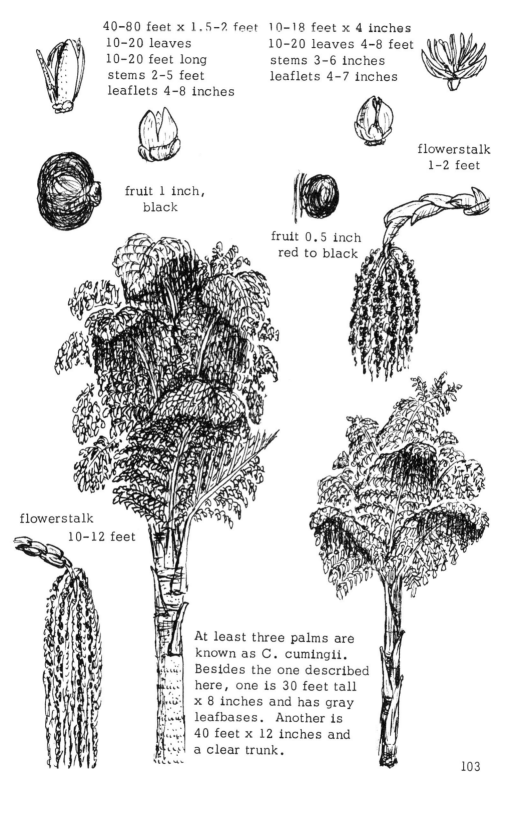

40-80 feet x 1.5-2 feet
10-20 leaves
10-20 feet long
stems 2-5 feet
leaflets 4-8 inches

10-18 feet x 4 inches
10-20 leaves 4-8 feet
stems 3-6 inches
leaflets 4-7 inches

flowerstalk
1-2 feet

fruit 1 inch,
black

fruit 0.5 inch
red to black

flowerstalk
10-12 feet

At least three palms are
known as C. cumingii.
Besides the one described
here, one is 30 feet tall
x 8 inches and has gray
leafbases. Another is
40 feet x 12 inches and
a clear trunk.

103

PINNATE LEAF PALMS
INDUPLICATE LEAFLETS

ARENGA

The genus contains 6 to 11 species, as the precise number is an unsettled question, from India westward to the Philippines. Four species are grown here.

Old leafstem bases and coarse black fibers cover the trunks of some species, while others are nearly clean and are ringed. Of the four species described, one has a solitary trunk, the others are multiple.

The leaves are pinnate, the leaflets folded with the midrib lower than the margins. The underside of the leaflets is light, in some species silvery. The leaves end in a large terminal leaflet. Margins of the leaflets are furnished with few to many sharp projections, in a distinct pattern for each species, and the tips are many pointed.

Arengas bloom at sucessive ring-scars from the top down, and then die. The flower stalk pushes its way through 5 to 7 bracts, and developes a number of simple branches with two large male flowers beside one female. The males ripen first and soon fall. The fruit is thin skinned and pulpy, with corrosive crystals that can irritate sensitive skin.

ARENGA PINNATA   Black Sugar Palm
The trunk is solitary, wrapped in nearly indestructible black fiber and large triangular leafstem bases. Leaves are rigid, held well above the horizontal. The leaflets are long and strap-like, occasionally eared, dark green above and almost silvery beneath. A few jagged points appear on the margins, and many at the tip. Leaflets are thin and fray easily, often showing a ragged appearance. More than half the leaflets are borne in bundles of 2 to 5, each pointing in a different direction. Male flowers are purple black. The fruit, which takes 2 years to ripen, is yellow brown. The tree begins to bloom when 10-12 years old.

5-8 feet
x 3 inches
8 leaves 7-8
feet long, on
stems 3 feet
120 leaflets
16-20 inches
x 1.25 inch
flower
stalk 18
inches
fruit 1
inch
red

20-50 feet x 18 inches
24 leaves 18-30
feet long
stems 5-6
feet
120-200
leaflets
5 feet
x 2-3
inches

6-12 feet x
12-18 inches
8-10 leaves
7-13 feet long

stems 30 inches
70-120 leaflets
30 x 1.2 inches
flowerstalk 4 feet
fruit 0.5 inch
red

Arenga englerii   Arenga pinnata   Arenga tremula

107

ARENGA   (continued)

ARENGA ENGLERI

Two to many clustered stems, covered with a black fiber and old leafstems and less than 10 feet tall, bear the arching leaves. The one-planed leaflets display prominent groups of sharp points along the margins. The leaflets are dark green above and silvery beneath, and are eared. The flower stalks are short, and are hidden within the leaves. The fruit changes through green to orange to red. This species has been here in South Florida longer than the one below, but may be in the process of being replaced by it, as some nurserymen report that they have more success in germinating seeds and in raising the seedlings of the newer palm.

ARENGA TREMULA

Two to many clustered stems, clean and ringed and less than 12 feet tall, support the arching leaves. The leaflets are narrower than those of A. engleri, and are much less likely to be eared. They are dark to medium green above and pale, rather than silvery, beneath. Some of the leaflets near the base are borne in groups of 2 or 3. They have a few small and inconspicuous points along the margins. The flower stalks tower over the plant. The fruit is white, turning red.

ARENGA MICROCARPA

Two to several thick, ringed stems, clean of fiber, cluster at the base, and may reach 20 to 30 feet in height. The leaflets are dark green and glossy above, dull silvery beneath, once ranked, with sharp projections mostly in the final third of the total length, and with prominent ears. The flowers are purple.

flowerstalk
7 feet

fruit 0.5 inch
red

20-30 x 1 foot
20-30 feet x 1 foot
15 leaves 15 feet
stems 5-6 feet
70 leaflets
30 x 2.5
inches

WALLICHIA

In addition to the one Wallichia that has been successfully introduced into South Florida, 5 other species
are known, from India and Malaysia. The one member
of the genus that we now have is uncommon here, but
it is unforgettable. It is at home in the Himalaya
Mountains, at 2,000 feet above sea level. The other
Wallichias are reported to be trunkless.

WALLICHIA DISTICHA   Wallich Palm
The trunk is of medium height or less, and is buried
beneath layers of gray and black fiber and triangular
leafstem bases. Before the fiber and the old leafstem
bases decay, the short-lived tree generally dies.

The leaves, on opposite sides of the tree, are long
and stiffly arching. The leaflets are long, growing in
bundles of 3 and 4 along the stem at 2 to 6 inch intervals. They are folded with the margins higher than the
midrib, and are dark to yellow green above, pale gray
beneath, and do not have ears. The margins produce
several groups of points from the midpoint of the leaflet to the blunt, jagged tip.

As with the Caryotas and the Arengas, Wallich Palms
reach maturity before flowering (10-15 years), bloom
and set fruit (4 to 6 years), and then die. Male flowers
occur alone near the tip of the flowerstalk, while two
may accompany one female near the base, where all of
the female flowers are found.

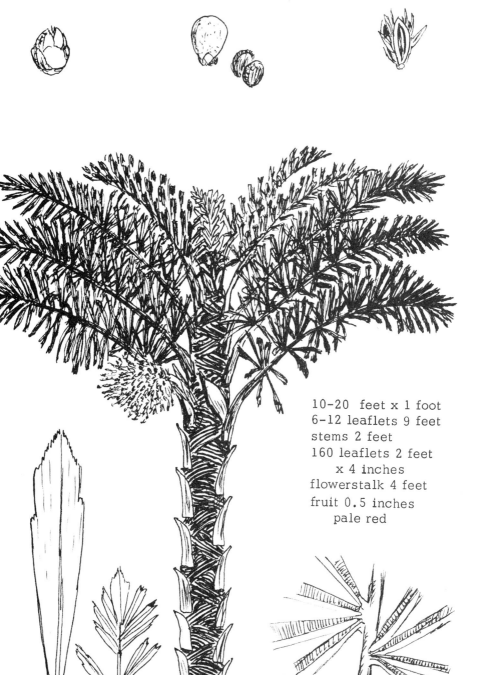

10-20 feet x 1 foot
6-12 leaflets 9 feet
stems 2 feet
160 leaflets 2 feet
   x 4 inches
flowerstalk 4 feet
fruit 0.5 inches
   pale red

PHOENIX

Tropical Africa and Asia contain 17 species of Phoenix, each in its own geographical region and habitat. When removed from these, and grown close together, the species hybridize freely, the crosses are fertile, and the progeny exhibit characters derived from each parent. This is precisely what has happened in South Florida to the 6 species herein discussed, making it advisable to refer to each Phoenix as a type -- as, a reclinata type, a canariensis type -- rather than commit a possibly erroneous identification.

Trunks are solitary with some species, and multiple with others. The surfaces are very rough, composed of old leafstem bases in spiral patterns crowded upon
(continued on page 114)

PHOENIX CANARIENSIS Canary Island Date
The massive, solitary trunk is often wider near the crown than near the base. The crown itself is much wider than the trunk, filled out with old leafstems and fiber, often tenanted with ferns and other plants. The base may produce a large above-ground root mass as the tree ages. The leaves are stiffly arched, holding the short, dull green leaflets slightly above the horizontal. The leaflets are several planed, but the angle between the ranks is small. The leafstems are twisted, sometimes to 90 degrees. Leaflets are stiff and sharp pointed. Flower stalks are bright orange, and highly visible. The fruit is edible, but is not considered to be a delicacy.

The Canary Island Date has been a valued landscape palm in South Florida for nearly 100 years, and many fine specimens are to be found in the older parts of our cities. Lack of trace elements can cause the leaflet tips to become yellow; spraying corrects this.

40-60 feet
x 2-4 feet

50-100 leaves 20 feet
stems 5 feet

320 leaflets 1.5 feet x 1 inch
flowerstalk 3 feet
fruit 0.75 inch, yellow

113

each other. The leafbases are not sheathing, and no crownshaft is present. Old trees are often thickened at the base by root masses.

The leafstems do not have marginal teeth, but the leaflets nearest the trunk are modified into thin, sharp spines (leafspines). The leaflets are induplicate (the margins higher than the midrib) and may be once or several ranked. Each leaf ends with one terminal leaflet. Leaflet margins are straight, smooth, and are not ribbed. The tips are sharply pointed, though often worn and frayed with age.

Flowers of each sex are normally borne on different trees. The flower stalks develope among the leaves,
(continued on page 116)

PHOENIX RECLINATA   Senegal Date
Normally producing multiple trunks (20 or more), the Senegal Date can be pruned of suckers and kept solitary. The trunk is much more slender than that of the Date, and the tree is taller than either the Rupicola or the Pygmy. The trunk is at first hidden in old leafstems and fiber matting, in middle age with the pointed remnants of the old leafstems, and in old age clean with ring-scars on top of swollen woody tissue. Leafstems are long, on some trees a bright orange, in others with orange patches, and they have more and longer spines than do the other date species. The leaflets are dark green, one planed and evenly spaced near the tip, in twos and threes at the midpoint, and, near the base of the leaf, two ranked. The spathes on some trees are bright orange.

This is still another species that has long been established in South Florida, and is quite common. The wide range of variation in Reclinatas is indicative of the amount of hybridization with other date species.

200-260 leaflets
1.5 feet
   x 1.75 inches
flowerstalk 3 feet
fruit 0.5, scarlet

30-40 feet
x 6-8 inches
25-50 leaves
15 feet long
stems 4 feet

115

with one papery bract splitting on the side away from
the trunk and soon falling. The long, flattened stalk
broadens at the tip, where the many simple branches
are attached. The flowers are small and stemless.
The fruit has a sweet, edible pulp between the thin
skin and the hard, grooved seed.

The parasitic fungus Ganoderma is known to prey on
several, and possibly all, species of date palms.

PHOENIX ROEBELENII   Pygmy Date, Roebeleni

This is ths smallest of the dates in common use here
in South Florida at this time. The trunk is usually solitary, though one individual in a thousand may produce
suckers; in other parts of the world, the species will
usually have multiple trunks. The remains of the old
leafstems wear to a series of spiralled knobs. A thick
matting envelopes the trunk below the crown. The leafstems are seldom twisted, but are very thin and pliable.
Leaflets are dark green and glossy, horizontal near the
stem, but flattened, flexible, and drooping at the midpoint, and are all in the same plane.

PHOENIX DACTYLIFERA   Date Palm

When allowed to, Date Palms have multiple trunks;
usually the suckers are removed and the trunk remains
solitary. The crown has little of the heavy matting of
the other dates. The gray leafstems are twisted only
slightly, and are very stiff. Leaflets are gray green,
coated with a fine powder. They are two ranked from
the tip to near the base, where they become four ranked, with relatively even spacing throughout.

Dates are not numerous in South Florida, largely because the trees will not produce good fruit here. They
do best where the winters are the wet season and the
summers are dry.

flowerstalk 1.5 feet

fruit
0.5 inch

orange to black

8-10 feet
x 9 inches
50 leaves
5 feet long
stems 2 inches
100 leaflets
15 x 0.75 inch

40-120
feet x
1-2 feet
20-100
leaves
20 feet
stems
4 feet
240
leaflets
1.5 feet
x 1 inch
flower-
stalk
4 feet
fruit 3
inches,
orange
to red

117

PHOENIX RUPICOLA   Rupicola Date
The trunk is of moderate height and width, and the
pattern of old leafstem bases is variable. The crown
is swollen with fiber matting. The thin, green, and
flexible leafstems are twice the width of those of the
Pygmy Date, and most of them are twisted through 90
degrees or more. The leaves are about twice as long,
and are of a brighter green. The paper thin leaflets
are in one plane, not drooping, and moderately stiff.
The leaflet tips are sometimes frayed and split along
the center line.

Though it is rather rare in South Florida, this species
is considered by some palm fanciers to be the best of
the dates for landscape use. It is from northern India.

PHOENIX SYLVESTRIS   Wild Date, Date-Sugar Palm
The Wild Date is thought to be the ancestor of the
true Date Palm. Though similar in general appearance,
the Wild Date is solitary, lacks the powder on the leaflets, has smaller leaves, a shorter trunk, and leaflets
are grouped in two and threes. The cloak of old, dead
leafstem bases is very heavy.

The Wild Date is not common in our area, perhaps
because we have not learned to use its sap for sugar
and for an alcoholic beverage, as is done in India.

fruit 0.75
inch, yellow

flowerstalk
3 feet

30-50 feet
x 16-18 inches
100 leaves
10-15 feet
stems 3 feet
250 leaflets
6-18 x 1 inch
flowerstalk
2-3 feet
fruit 1 inch,
orange-yellow

15-25 feet
x 6-10 inches
50 leaves
10 feet long
stems 3 feet
200 leaflets
18 x 1 inch

119

PINNATE LEAF PALMS
REDUPLICATE

SPINY

ACROCOMIA

There are about 30 species of Acrocomia, from South America and the West Indies. Several have been tried in South Florida, and successfully. They fulfill the same purpose as the Royal Palm in landscaping, and deserve to be as popular. Once established, they are tolerant of adverse conditions, though susceptible to Ganoderma. They are often called Gru-gru palms.

The gray, solitary trunks are smooth and straight, sometimes with a slight bend, and often with a bulge above the middle. The presence and the amount of spines on the trunks are variable.

The broad leafstem bases are studded with spines, and others are scattered randomly along the leafstems. The leaflets are very numerous, and are several ranked. The leaflet tips are sharply pointed, and the leaflet margins are unribbed.

The flower stalk is large, with a woody, persistent spathe that is covered on the outside with small spines and a reddish brown fuzz. The stalk has many simple branches (186, in one specimen). The flowers of each sex are separate, with the females near the base and the males near the tip of the branches.

ACROCOMIA ACULEATA   Macaw Palm
The underside of the leaflets of this species is pale with tiny white hair. The trunk is smooth, spiny when young, often without spines in age, and sometimes is roughened with leafstem remnants.

ACROCOMIA TOTAI   Totai Palm
This species is slightly the smaller of the two. It has shorter leaves and flower stalks, and does not have the white hair on the underside of the leaflets. The ring-scars are raised at the point of attachment.

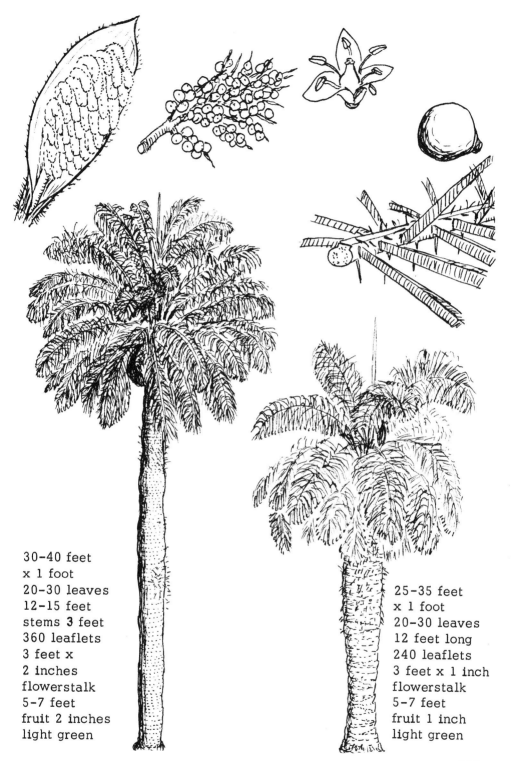

30-40 feet
x 1 foot
20-30 leaves
12-15 feet
stems 3 feet
360 leaflets
3 feet x
2 inches
flowerstalk
5-7 feet
fruit 2 inches
light green

25-35 feet
x 1 foot
20-30 leaves
12 feet long
240 leaflets
3 feet x 1 inch
flowerstalk
5-7 feet
fruit 1 inch
light green

123

GASTROCOCOS

The genus has only one member, native to the island
of Cuba, where the swollen trunk is sometimes used as
a watering trough. The tree is seldom encountered in
South Florida, although it does grow well here. It will
remain at the same height for years, perhaps gathering
its forces, and suddenly shoot up rapidly to attain its
full growth. The large spathe and the many yellow
flowers are quite showy.

GASTROCOCOS CRISPA   Cuban Belly Palm

The trunk is always bulging, in sharp contrast to the
rather slender base. The horizontal ring-scars are thin
and complete. On most trees, flat gray spines cover
the ring-scars, a series of half-inch bands of spines,
but some trees have very few spines on the trunk.

The very spiny leafstem bases are also covered with
waxy down. The leafstems are spiny, and even upper
surfaces and margins of the leaves of seedlings have
thin yellow bristles. The leaflets are a glossy green
above, a blue green beneath, and are crowded together
along the leafstem. The tips are sharp, but wear away
to a blunt point. The margins are not ribbed.

The flower stalk is long, and grows among the lower
leaves of the crown. The woody and persistent spathe
is covered with spines and a reddish fuzz. The male
flowers are borne at the tip ends of the simple branches,
the females near the base.

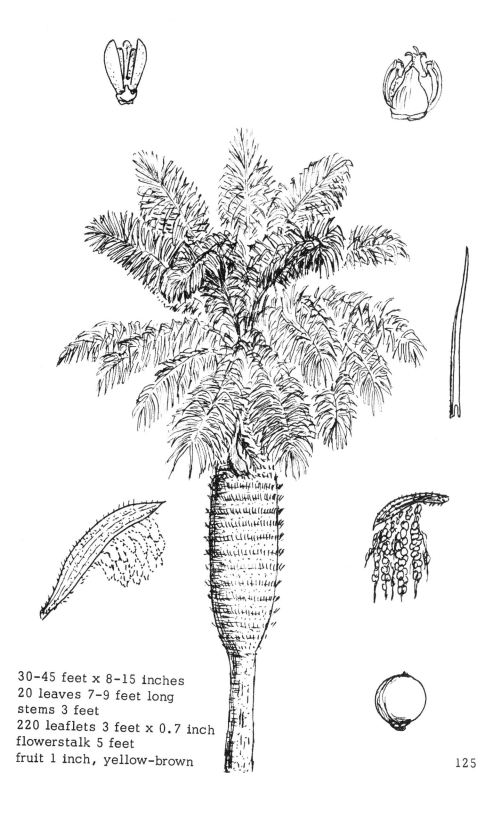

30-45 feet x 8-15 inches
20 leaves 7-9 feet long
stems 3 feet
220 leaflets 3 feet x 0.7 inch
flowerstalk 5 feet
fruit 1 inch, yellow-brown

125

AIPHANES

South America and the islands of the Caribbean are the home of the Aiphanes genus, where some 40 species have been described. The armament of these palms has kept them from the popularity they deserve.

The trunks are solitary and light in color, with sharp light gray to black spines that are flattened at the base. The ring-scars are complete and sharply ridged, with rows of spines growing upon them. Aerial roots may or may not be present.

Spines occur on the leafstem bases and leafstems all the way to the tip of the leaf, and often on the midribs of the leaflets. The leaflets, in one plane, are short and wide, with jagged tips.

Flower stalks are long and narrow, with spines on the spathe. Each stalk has one set of branches. The flowers are white to yellow, with the males near the tip and the females near the base of the branch. The clusters of red fruit are very ornamental.

AIPHANES ACANTHOPHYLLA   Coyure Palm
The leaflets are widest near their midpoint, tapering to a broad tip with many jagged points. The species is fast growing. It is from Puerto Rico.

AIPHANES CARYOTAEFOLIA   Chonta Palm
The ruffled leaflets expand in width as they grow farther from the leafstem. Each leaflet tip has three major points and many minor ones. The palm comes from northern South America.

Another palm of this genus, A. erosa, is rare in this area. It is taller, with a trunk 9 inches wide, and has spines that can be as much as 9 inches long.

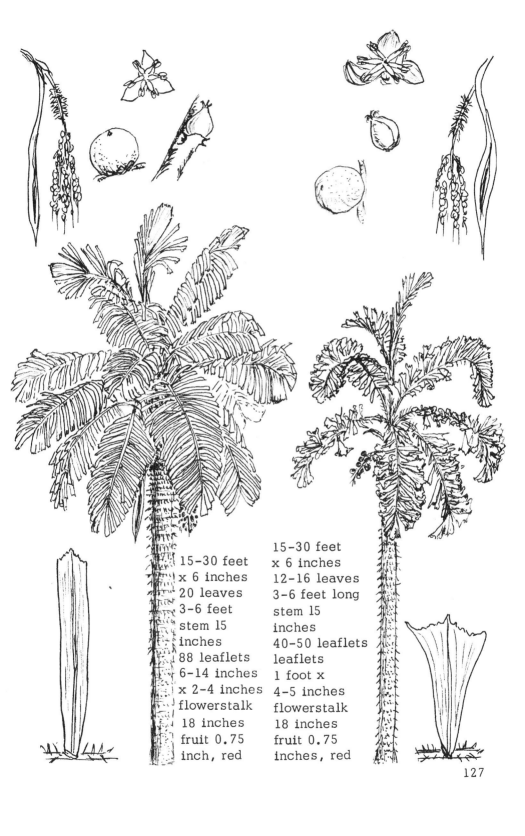

15-30 feet
x 6 inches
20 leaves
3-6 feet
stem 15
inches
88 leaflets
6-14 inches
x 2-4 inches
flowerstalk
18 inches
fruit 0.75
inch, red

15-30 feet
x 6 inches
12-16 leaves
3-6 feet long
stem 15
inches
40-50 leaflets
leaflets
1 foot x
4-5 inches
flowerstalk
18 inches
fruit 0.75
inches, red

BACTRIS

Only a very few of the 200 or more species of Bactris palms have been brought here from South America. Of these, the two species below have done the best.

The multiple trunks have sheaths that are persistent, thin, papery, and spined; beneath them lie new spines ready to assume a horizontal position when the sheath falls. The ring-scars are complete and widely spaced.

The leafstems are at least partly spiny, and have no flocking or down. The leaflet margins are spiny in one species. The leaflet tips are sharply pointed.

The flower stalks are thick, with one set of branches. The spathe is leathery, not woody, and quite spiny. Flowers contain both sex organs.

BACTRIS GASIPAES   Peach Palm
Five or six light brown trunks are normal for a Peach Palm, but solitary trees may be created by pruning the suckers. The large spines are well scattered between the ring-scars. The leafstems are spined only at the base. Young leaves may be undivided, with the leaflets separating as the leaf ages. The leaflets attach to the stem in groups of 2 to 5, and are several ranked, lacking marginal spines. Terminal leaflets may have several midribs. The fruit is edible, and is featured in native markets in Central America.

BACTRIS MAJOR   Lata Palm
The many trunks are thin, smooth, light brown, and spined. The sheaths are also spined, and are darker than the trunk beneath. The leaflets are in one plane, with tiny spines set along the edges. The terminal leaflets have one midrib each.

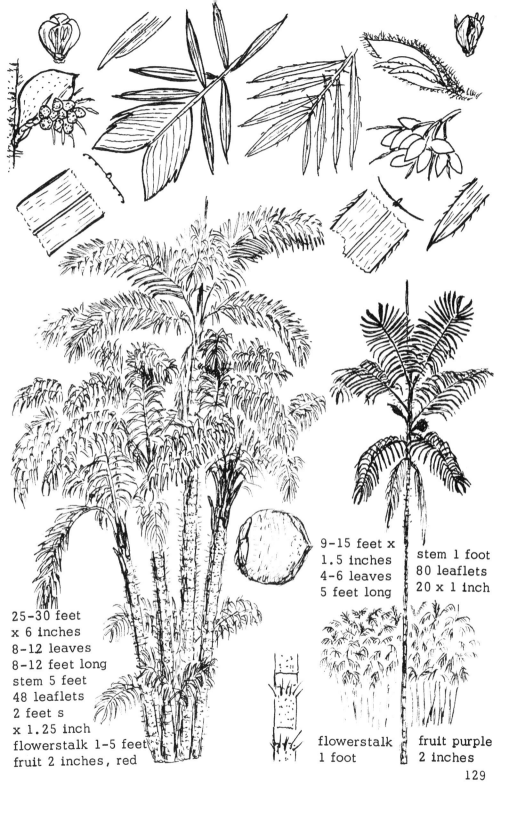

25-30 feet
x 6 inches
8-12 leaves
8-12 feet long
stem 5 feet
48 leaflets
2 feet s
x 1.25 inch
flowerstalk 1-5 feet
fruit 2 inches, red

9-15 feet x
1.5 inches
4-6 leaves
5 feet long

stem 1 foot
80 leaflets
20 x 1 inch

flowerstalk
1 foot

fruit purple
2 inches

129

ASTROCARYUM

Of the 50 or more species in this genus from Mexico and Central America, only a few have been brought to South Florida. The one species discussed herein is by no means common. The prickly nature of these palms probably accounts for their lack of popularity.

ASTROCARYUM MEXICANUM

The trunk is solitary, with the close-set ring-scars supporting flat, vicious spines. There is little fiber in the crown, and no crownshaft.

The leafstems are gray and spiny. The leaflets are in one plane and flat, with those at the tip in a group of 10 or more, those nearest the base in a group of 5 or more, with most of the remaining leaflets appearing singly -- though some leaves will have another group about midway between the other two. The upper side of the leaflets is dark green and the underside is a blend of green and silver. The leaflet tips are sharply pointed, and the margins are not ribbed.

The flower stalk is surmounted by a short, spined spathe. Flowers and fruit are crowded into one spiny mass, with the males on slender projecting branches, the females and the fruit in clusters near the base.

15-25 feet x 4 inches
20 leaves 10 feet long
stems 30 inches
80 ribs 30 inches long
flowerstalk 15 inches
fruit 1.5 inch, brown

131

PINNATE LEAF PALMS

REDUPLICATE

CROWNSHAFT

HYOPHORBE

Four species form this genus, from the Mascarene
Islands in the Indian Ocean. Two of them like the
South Florida conditions, and, though not common,
are gaining acceptance. They are very tolerant of
drought, salty soil, and even neglect. Young plants
make excellent potted specimens.

The solitary, gray brown trunks are shaped somewhat
like spindles or bottles, and are clean, except when
young and small. The ring-scars are close, 1 to 2
inches, and do not protrude.

The leafstems are stiffly arched, unarmed, twisted,
and carry the leaflets almost to the trunk. The leaflets
are held in a V, their points of attachment broad and
swollen so that they touch near the tip of the leaf.
The margins are not ribbed, and the tips are pointed
sharply. There are no reins.

The flower stalks are borne below the leaves, the 8
papery bracts rolled tightly around a cigar-shaped mass
of stalk, branches, and branchlets. The flowers grow
in groups (acervuli) of 4 to 6 males to one female. The
males mature and fall before the female opens.

HYOPHORBE VERSCHAFFELTII   Spindle Palm
The Spindle Palm is narrow at the base and widest at
the crown. The trunk is light brown and smooth, with
the ring-scars making dark bands. The leaflets are in
several ranks, do not have secondary ribs, and are
stiff to the midpoint, moderately lax beyond it.

HYOPHORBE REVAUGHNII/LAGENICAULIS   Bottle Palm
The Bottle Palm is widest at the base, and tapers to
a narrow neck. The leaflets, in the same plane, are
stiff, and have a set of secondary ribs. Two species
names are in common use for the same plant.
Until very recently, the genus name was Mascarena.

20-35 feet x 1.5 feet
6-8 leaves 9-10 feet
stems 1 foot
100-160 leaflets
32 x 2 inches
flowerstalk 30 inches
fruit 0.5 inch, black

12-15 feet x 2 feet
6-8 leaves 9-12 feet
stems 9 inches
140 leaflets
27 x 2 inches
flowerstalk 30 inches
fruit 1 inch, black

SATAKENTIA

One of the latest introductions to the palm flora of South Florida, the Satake Palm seems assured of a good reception. It is an attractive, clean looking palm in the medium height range, resembling the Royal Palms but smaller, more slender, and with a darker trunk. It is from the Ryukyu Islands, the chain that stretches from Taiwan (Formosa) to Japan.

SATAKENTIA LIUKIUENSIS   Satake Palm
The trunk is solitary, a very light brown marked with shallow vertical fissures of a darker brown, and set on a slightly bulbous base. The ring-scars are prominent, darker than the trunk, but smooth, in the same plane. The crownshaft has a long, bright green sheath, split down the back, the sides of the tear turning brown.

The leaves are glossy bright green on both sides, on leafstems that are not twisted. Reins are present on some leaves, but not on all. The leaflets are rather lax, in one plane, and have smooth, ribbed margins and sharply pointed tips. The surface of the leaflet is not flat, but is pleated, or slightly folded. One or more of the leaflets at the tip may have two midribs, but not in every case. Secondary ribs mark the under side.

The flowerstalk appears below the crownshaft, and divides into branches and branchlets. Male floral organs are in separate flowers from those with female organs, and occur in triads of two males and one female flower.

20-30 feet x 8 inches
10-13 leaves 12 feet long
stems 20 inches
120 leaflets 2 feet x 1.5 inches
fruit 0.5 inches, red

ARCHONTOPHOENIX

Two of the three species in this Australian genus do fairly well in our area. They seem to be prone to a trace element deficiency, a reason that some nurserymen use for not stocking them.

These are tall, solitary palms, with the crownshafts longer and thinner than those of the Dictyospermas. The trunks of younger specimens are brown; with age, the color wears to a light gray. The ring-scars leave prominent steps that encircle the trunk. The base of most individuals of this genus is swollen.

The leaves are dark green, stiffly arched on twisted stems. Reins hang from the lowest leaflets. Margins of the leaflets are not ribbed, but two or more sets of secondary ribs project on the under side, while the midrib is raised above the upper surface. The leaflets, in one plane, are arched in cross section. The tip of each leaflet is pinched in to form a spine.

Two papery green bracts enclose the flower stalk, growing below the crownshaft. The stalks are sturdy, with branches and branchlets. Two large and showy male flowers border one female blossom.

ARCHONTOPHOENIX ALEXANDRAE   Alexandra Palm
The swollen base below a narrow trunk is a characteristic of the species. The leaflets, held in a slight V, are gray on the under side, and the interior ribs are prominent. The flowers are white to green.

ARCHONTOPHOENIX CUNNINGHAMIANA   King Palm
The base is less swollen in this species, and the tree is shorter. Leaflets are dark green on both sides and are more relaxed, with the interior ribs less prominent, than in the above. The midribs have strands of wooly scales on the under side. The flowers are lilac to lavender.

0.5 inch

coral

50-100 feet
  x 6-8 inches
8-12 leaves
  8-12 inches long
stems 4-12 inches
100-150 leaflets
    3 feet x 2 inches
flowerstalk 3 feet
fruit 0.5 inch, red

40-80 feet
  x 8 inches
8-12 leaves
  8-10 feet long
stems 4-8 inches
120 leaflets
   30 x 2-4 inches
flowerstalk
   30 inches

139

DICTYOSPERMA

Both species of this genus, from the Mascarene Islands, have become common in South Florida gardens. They are often called Hurricane Palms, as they withstand high winds better than most other palms. Slow to grow, they are very difficult to transplant.

The solitary trunk is straight, on a swollen base, with ring-scars forming steps, and with numerous vertical fissures. The wide crownshaft is prominent, a light green covered with gray to tan waxy scales.

The leafstems twist 90 degrees, so that leaflets at the leaftip parallel the trunk. Leaves are shiny dark green on both sides, usually with long reins. Leaflets are in one plane, with the margins heavily ribbed and with twisted brown scales under the midrib. The leaflet tips are sharply pointed.

The undeveloped flowers are protected by two flat, papery, golden-brown bracts, one inside the other. The stalk is short and thick, with one set of branches, and is borne beneath the crown of leaves. There are two male flowers beside each female.

DICTYOSPERMA ALBUM   Princess Palm
The taller and more common of the two species, the Princess Palm has a smoother trunk, usually gray. Its leaves are longer, and its leaflets longer, wider, and more numerous. The flowers are reddish yellow. A variety, D. album var. rubrum, shows reddish veins in the leaves of young trees.

DICTYOSPERMA AUREUM   Yellow Princess Palm
This species is smaller, less common, and has a darker trunk with raised ring-scars. Leaves of young plants often have bright orange veins. The flowers are white and yellow.

25-40 feet x 8 inches
15-20 leaves 8-12 feet long
stems 6-12 inches
120 leaflets 3 feet x 2-3 inches
flowerstalk 15-24 inches
fruit 0.5 inch, purple black

20-25 feet x
6 inches
15-20 leaves
8 feet long
stems 1-2 feet
100 leaflets
30 x 1.5
inches
flowerstalk
20 inches
fruit 1 inch
purple black

141

VEITCHIA

The South Sea Islands -- the Philippines, the Fijis,
New Caledonia, and New Hebrides -- have given us
the Veitchias. Of the 10 or so species, one has been
known and prized in South Florida for many years, and
known for most of that time as Adonidia merrillii. The
genus Adonidia has been discarded, and this species
placed with the Veitchias. Nevertheless, there are a
number of characteristics of V. merrillii that differ so
greatly from those of the other Veitchias that it is not
easy to generalize on them all. For this reason, I
have chosen to treat these newcomers on another page.

VEITCHIA MERRILLII Adonidia, Manila, Christmas Palm
The trunk is solitary, the surface dark with ring-scars
crowded several to the inch where the tree grows in full
sun, or smooth and gray with ring-scars 1 to 2 inches
apart where the tree is grown in the shade. In any case,
the crownshaft is prominent, rather short and thick, and
the base of the trunk is swollen.

The leafstems are stiffly arched, holding the leaves
well above the horizontal, and are not twisted. At the
base of the leaf, the leaflets are in several planes,
while those at the midpoint and the tip are in one plane,
held in a narrow V. The leaflet margins are ribbed, and
the tips taper to a slender but jagged point. Most of
the leaves have reins.

Two papery bracts envelope the undeveloped flower
stalk; these fall before it unfolds. The white flowers
appear at the nodes, or joints, of the branchlets, two
males to each female on the lower portion, males only
toward the tip.

10-25 feet x
  10 inches
9-15 leaves
  6 feet long
100 leaflets
  18-30 x 2
  inches
flowerstalk
  2 feet
fruit 1.5 inch,
  red

143

VEITCHIA   (continued)

The remaining Veitchias are nearly identical in appearance. The trunks are smooth and gray, the light ring-scars 4 to 6 inches apart, the bases swollen.

The leafstems arch gracefully and are not twisted. The leaflets are in a plane and are not held in a V. Margins are ribbed, and the tips jagged, turning to a pale brown and dying back. Tufts of wooly scales occur at the top of the crownshaft, and some species have nearly transparent scales along the nerves on the underside of the leaflets.

The flowerstalks are exceptionally thick and sturdy, rather short, and have branches and branchlets. There are two papery bracts that fall early. In two species, old flowerstalks are marked on the trunk by fibers.

Veitchia winin -- lower leaves slightly below horizontal; wooly scales gray; leaflet scales present; tufts of fiber present; 45-65 feet x 10 inches; 8-10 leaves 15 feet long; 120 leaflets 24 x 3 inches; fruit 0.5 inch.
Veitchia montgomeryana -- lower leaves held at horizontal; wooly scales black; leaflet scales present; fiber tufts absent; 25-40 feet x 8 inches; 8-10 leaves 10 feet long; 120-140 leaflets 18 x 3; fruit 1.5 inch.
Veitchia joannis -- lower leaves droop below horizontal; wooly scales pale brown; leaflet scales absent; fiber tufts absent; 35-50 feet x 9 inches; 8-10 leaves 10 feet long; 140-160 leaflets 18 x 2.5; fruit 1.5 inch.
Veitchia arecina -- lower leaves slightly below horizontal; wooly scales gray; leaflet scales absent; fiber tufts absent; 20-30 feet x 6 inches; 8-10 leaves 8 feet long; 90 leaflets 24 x 3 inches; fruit 1 inch.
Veitchia mcdanielsii -- lower leaves held above the horizontal; wooly scales black; leaflet scales present; 15-25 feet x 6 inches; 8-10 leaves 9 feet long; 74 leaflets 18 x 4 inches; fruit not available.

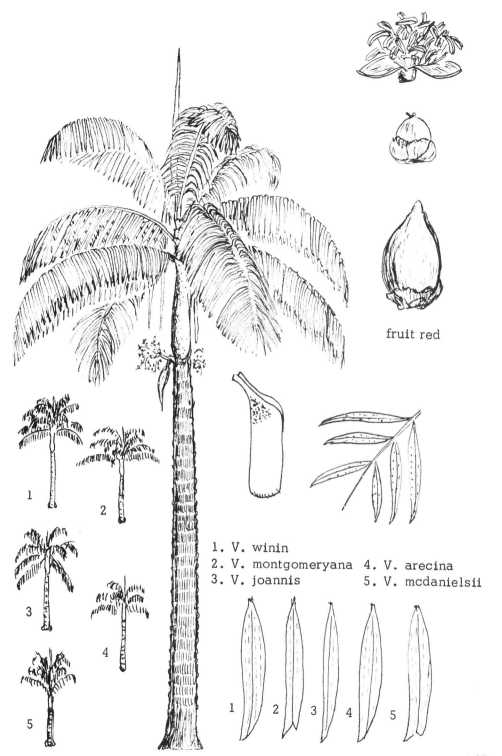

fruit red

1. V. winin
2. V. montgomeryana   4. V. arecina
3. V. joannis   5. V. mcdanielsii

145

CARPENTARIA

At present a little known palm from Australia, this
species is a newcomer of great promise. It takes full
sun, and apparently has no particular requirements in
soil quality.

CARPENTARIA ACUMINATA

The trunk is solitary, smooth, and gray brown, with
shallow vertical fissures of darker brown. The crownshaft is long, with the sheathing base of the lowest
leaf split down the back. The ring-scars are as much
as 10 inches apart, causing the leafstems to be that
distance from one another, and thereby elongating the
crown. The base is not swollen.

The leafstems are moderately stiff, and do not twist.
The leaves are medium green on both sides. The leaflets are in a plane, held in a V, with smooth unribbed
margins and tips that are cut into 4 points, turning to a
straw color and dying back with age. The terminal pair
of leaflets each have 2 to 6 large ribs.

The flower stalk, growing below the crown, has 2
bracts. The stem branches twice. Two male flowers
guard a central female, but bloom and fall well before
the female opens.

25-40 feet x 8 inches
12 leaves 6 feet long, stems 4-12 inches
108 leaflets 2 feet x 1.5 inches
flowerstalk 4 feet
fruit 0.5 inch, crimson to black

147

BRASSIOPHOENIX

Only one species of this genus has been discovered
in the tropical forests of northern Australia. The genus
is not well enough known, at this time, for the certain
assignment of names; so the indicator of doubt, the
letters "sp.," must be used instead of a species name.
Despite this, the palm appears to thrive in the South
Florida climate, when planted in partial shade and pro-
vided with plenty of water. It is still rare here.

BRASSIOPHOENIX SP.   (possibly B. drymophloeoides)
    The solitary trunk is straight and slender, light brown
near the base, tending to light green near the crown.
The crownshaft is slender and fairly long (18 inches.)

The leafstems are scurfy, dotted with small curls of
black wool, and are not twisted. The leaflets are triangular, with 3 major points and many minor ones. The
margins are strongly ribbed. The terminal leaflets are
condensations of several leaflets, with a variable number of ribs.

Several bracts surround the undeveloped flower stalk,
borne below the crown. The stalk is stout, with less
than 10 branches, some of which branch again. Flowers
are in threes, two males around one female.

20 feet x 2.5 inches
6 leaves 5 feet long
stems 4-6 inches
16-20 leaflets 20 x 6 inches
flower stalk 1 foot
fruit 0.3 inch, white
   to orange

149

DRYMOPHLOEUS

About a dozen members of this genus have been discovered in northern Australia and the nearby islands. Two of them have been introduced into South Florida, but are seldom seen as yet. They are very good palms for shaded locations, but they cannot stand full sun, and they must be protected from cold, dry winds.

The trunks are solitary and smooth, gray green or brown with ring-scars of a darker brown. The crownshaft is short and narrow. There is no fiber.

The leaves are few, from 3 to 6. The leaflets, in one plane, are dark green and strongly ribbed, both in the center and on the margins, and triangular, with broad tips that have many jagged points. The terminal leaflets have several midribs, indicating that a number of leaflets have been condensed into one.

The flower stalks are very short, and have few branches. There are two bracts, one splitting along the top, the other along the side. The flowers are green and very small, two males to one female.

DRYMOPHLOEUS OLIVAEFORMIS   Olive Palm
The Olive Palm is the shorter of the two, and also the least common. The trunk is thinner, and the wood is softer than in the following species. The terminal leaflet is one continuous tissue across the tip of the leaf. The outer surface of the fruit is wrinkled, and the seed covering is smooth around the seed.

DRYMOPHLOEUS BEGUINII   Beguine Palm
The Beguine Palm is the taller, with a thicker trunk and much harder wood. The terminal leaflets are not connected. The outer surface of the fruit is smooth, and the seed covering folds down into the seed.

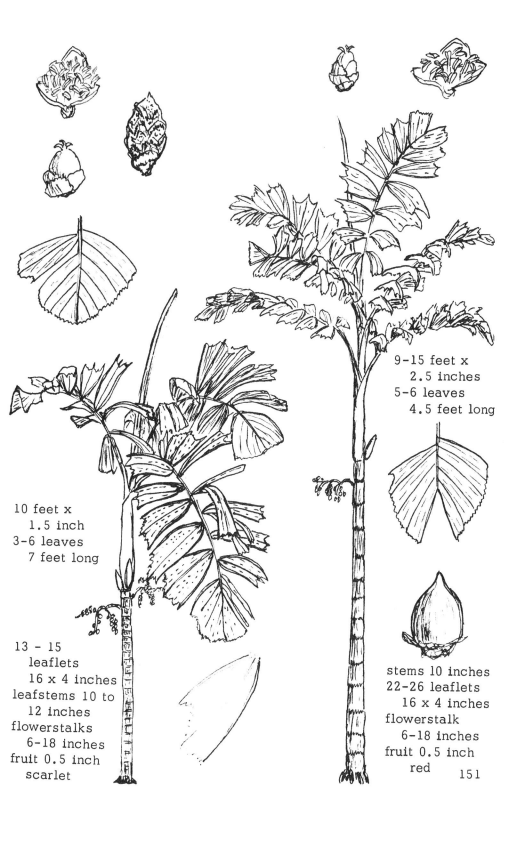

9-15 feet x
2.5 inches
5-6 leaves
4.5 feet long

10 feet x
1.5 inch
3-6 leaves
7 feet long

13 - 15
leaflets
16 x 4 inches
leafstems 10 to
12 inches
flowerstalks
6-18 inches
fruit 0.5 inch
scarlet

stems 10 inches
22-26 leaflets
16 x 4 inches
flowerstalk
6-18 inches
fruit 0.5 inch
red

151

PTYCHOSPERMA

Forty one species of this genus are known, from New Guinea, the Solomon Islands, and northern Australia. One species with a solitary trunk and one with multiple trunks are widespread in South Florida, and another, a recent importation with multiple trunks, is beginning to make its way here. All need partial shade when young.

These are palms of less than average height (to 30 feet), with slender, smooth, ringed, light gray trunks.

Leaves are few (6 to 10), with some of them twisted, and all rather stiffly arched. Leaflets are in a plane, the margins ribbed, the tips blunt and jagged. There are no reins in palms of this genus.

The two bracts are green and papery, and soon fall. The stalk, below the crown, branches twice. Flowers are white, and rather large for palm blossoms. There are two male flowers for each female.

PTYCHOSPERMA ELEGANS   Solitaire Palm
The Solitaire Palm has a single trunk with a swollen base and raised ring-scars, 1 to 4 inches apart, on a gray surface. The leaves are stiffly arched, with the leaflets held above the horizontal. Each leaflet has 5 or more pleats, and is green above, gray below. It is one of the best palms for smaller yards, thriving in sites that are protected from cold, dry winds.

PTYCHOSPERMA MACARTHURII   Macarthur Palm
The multiple trunks are light gray, with raised ring-scars. The leafstems are less rigid than those of the Solitaire Palm, are without pleats, are more relaxed, and are of the same color on both sides. This is one of the long-time Florida favorites. It can contract the parasitic fungus Ganoderma.

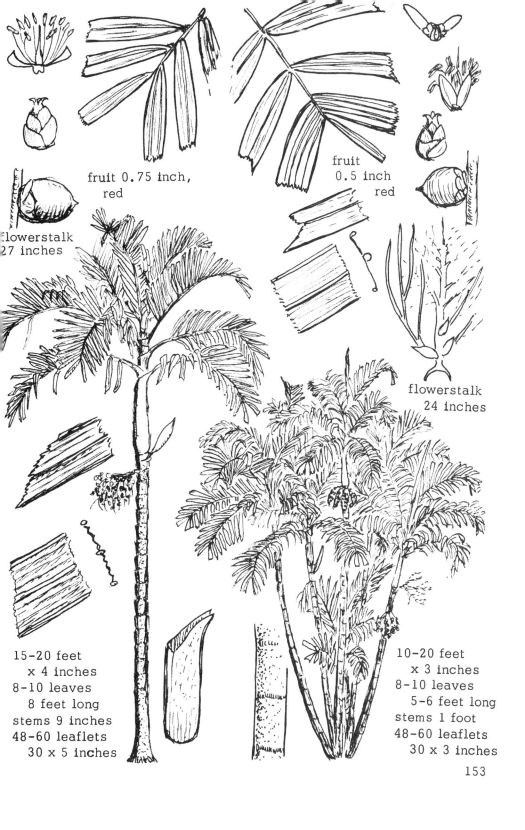

fruit 0.75 inch,
red

fruit
0.5 inch
red

flowerstalk
27 inches

flowerstalk
24 inches

15-20 feet
   x 4 inches
8-10 leaves
   8 feet long
stems 9 inches
48-60 leaflets
   30 x 5 inches

10-20 feet
   x 3 inches
8-10 leaves
   5-6 feet long
stems 1 foot
48-60 leaflets
   30 x 3 inches

153

PTYCHOSPERMA SANDERIANUM

Closely crowded multiple trunks support leaves that
are dark green on both sides. The leaflets are horizontal and flexible, very narrow, with tips that taper to a
jagged double point. Adult trees resemble the common
Chrysalidocarpus lutescens, but the leaflets are less
than half as wide and are without the yellow cast of the
latter species, and are held flat, not in a V.

This palm is another newcomer to South Florida, and
one that promises well. It is partial to shaded sites,
and should be hardened before planting in full sun.

An undetermined number of other Ptychospermas have
been brought to South Florida, arriving here well before
the difficult task of relating them to the rest of their
genus has been completed. Until this work has been
done, they must continue under the name of Ptychosperma species (Ptychosperma sp.), a poor apology for the
lack of a name of one's own. One of these, resembling
P. elegans but smaller, has black fruit. This unnamed
species is now being propagated and may become well
established before it is named.

Several other Ptychospermas are mentioned in the
chapter on additional palms.

15-20 feet x 1.5 inches
7-8 leaves 6 feet long
stems 12 inches
74 leaflets 18 x 0.5 inch
flowerstalk 14 inches
fruit 0.5 inch, red

HYDRIASTELE

The wet, warm tropics of Australia's northern coast
have produced the genus Hydriastele. Several species
are known to exist, but the exact number has not been
determined. They all seem to be understory palms, at
their best in partial shade and well-watered locations.
The only species in cultivation here is still very rare,
but it promises to become a welcome addition to our
palm flora. The specific name has not been determined
but it may well be rostrata, and that is the name under
which the palm is usually sold.

HYDRIASTELE ROSTRATA

A number of trunks (2 to 12 or more) arise and curve
from the center of the clump, each trunk light to dark
gray, marked with ring-scars from 2 to 4 inches apart.
The crownshafts are slender, grass green, dull, and
often roughened. The base of the trunk is not swollen.

The leafstems are not twisted. The leaflets are in
one plane, and are held in a slight V. They are curving,
but they do not bend. They are attached to the stem in
an irregular manner, sometimes in bunches. Each of
the terminal leaflets has several to 15 ribs, and is con-
siderably wider than the other leaflets. A few of the
leaflets back from the tip may have 2 ribs. The tips
are jagged, with many thin points. The margins are
not ribbed. A set of secondary ribs is often present.

The flower stalk is sheathed in two papery bracts.
In falling, these reveal a short, thick stalk with short
branches and thin branchlets that bear both male and
female flowers.

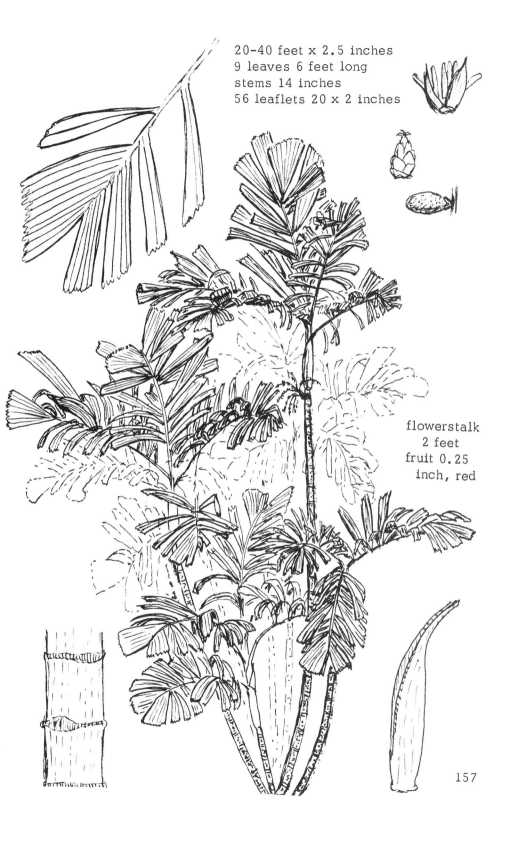

20-40 feet x 2.5 inches
9 leaves 6 feet long
stems 14 inches
56 leaflets 20 x 2 inches

flowerstalk
2 feet
fruit 0.25
inch, red

157

ROYSTONEA

About 17 species of Roystonea are found throughout
the Caribbean Basin, from Florida along the islands to
northern South America. Possibly 4 of them are now in
South Florida. One of these is fairly distinct, while
the others are so close in appearance as to make their
identification difficult, if not impossible, despite the
many schemes that have been advanced to that end.

All of them grow well in our area, and are a favorite
street planting tree in some communities. They withstand hurricanes quite well, as they shed the leaves,
to renew them after the storm has passed.

The solitary trunks are clean, smooth, nearly white,
and most impressive. The crownshafts are cylinders
of bright green, 5 to 6 feet high. Ring-scars, though
visible upon close inspection, are not prominent.

The sturdy leafstems are not twisted. Leaves are a
bright green on both sides. The leaflets are several
ranked, the margins not ribbed, the tips pointed.

Each flower stalk is enclosed in one massive bract,
green and ribbed on the outer side, white and smooth
on the interior. The stalk divides into branches and
branchlets. The tiny yellow green flowers grow in
threes, two males to each female.

ROYSTONEA OLERACEA   Caribee Royal

The trunk has no bulge, a feature that differentiates
this species from the other three immediately. There
is a very apparent taper to the trunk, with the portion
below the crown much narrower than the swollen base.
The leaves are longer than those of other Royals, and
arch above the horizontal, where those of all of the
other species hang below the crown. The leaflets are
two ranked; in other species, they are many ranked.

80-120 feet
x 43 inches
12-16 leaves
20-25 feet
370 leaflets
42 x 2 inches
stems 4-6 feet
flowerstalk
4 feet
fruit 1 inch
purple to
black

159

The other three species of Royals that are known to be here are very similar in general appearance, and may hybridize. The information given below is a condensation of the systems of several experts, and is given without any sort of guarantee.

R. oleracea differs from the other Royals in the lack of bulging of the trunk, in holding the lowest leaves above the horizontal, in the appearance of having the leaflets in one rank, and in having larger fruit.

R. borinquena can be distinguished from R. elata and R. regia by the dense crowding of the flowers (in this species they touch one another), by the small scales or hairs on the flowerstalks, and by the comparatively glossy upper surface of the leaflets. The oblong fruit is yellow brown. The species is native to Puerto Rico.

R. elata, the Florida species, has leaflets that are vaguely or not at all ribbed on either side of the midrib, flowerstalks that are long and loose, and purple (some authorities say "violet-purple") fruit nearly globular in shape, 0.3 x 0.5 inches.

R. regia, from Cuba, has leaflets that have a set of prominent secondary ribs on each side of the midrib, flowerstalks that are about as broad as long, and a red to purple fruit that is almost oblong, 0.25 x 0.5 inch. Most large Royals in South Florida cities were brought to this country from Cuba in the 1930's.

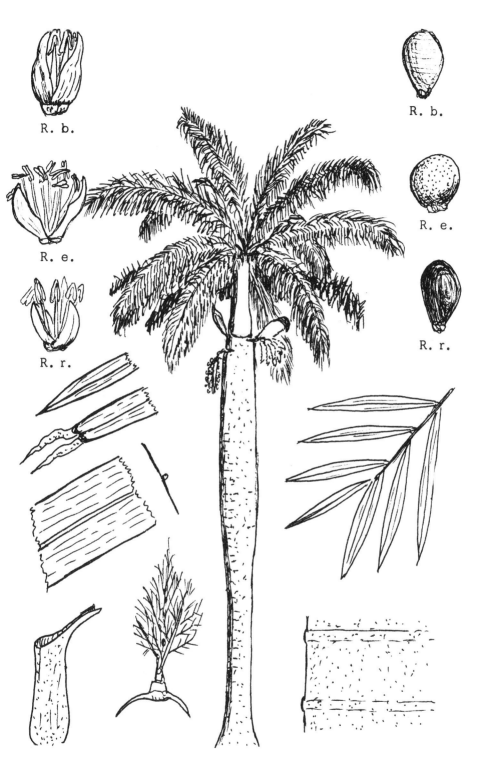

R. b.

R. e.

R. r.

R. b.

R. e.

R. r.

161

PSEUDOPHOENIX

The coastlines and the islands of the Caribbean are home to this genus, with two to four species strewn from the Florida keys to Panama. It is one of the most attractive of the native palms, hardy, disease resistant, and perfectly adapted by natural selection.

Trunks of younger specimens are gray green, with light brown ring-scars, and smooth; older trunks are dark gray, pitted and scarred, with silvery splinters. The amount and the location of bulging varies from one tree to another, and it is unusual to find an individual with a completely straight trunk. The crownshaft is short and wide, and quite prominent.

The leafstem bases are deeply notched in the back. The twisted leafstems are stout and gray green. The leaflets are rather stiff, with barely ribbed margins, sharp tips, and low, visibly detectable secondary ribs. In any leaf, the majority of the leaflets will be found to be sharing the same point of attachment with one or more others, each of them in a different plane.

The flower stalks appear within the leaves, with 2 roughened tubular bracts, and dividing into branches, branchlets, and sub-branchlets. The flowers are on short stems, usually with both sex organs.

PSEUDOPHOENIX SARGENTII   Buccaneer, Hog Palm
This species has the thinner trunk, with shorter and stiffer leaves, and a flower stalk with all its ramifications about as broad as it is long. The fruit is smaller. One of the 4 varieties of this species is native to the Bahamas, Elliott Key, and formerly Long Key.

PSEUDOPHOENIX VINIFERA   Cherry Palm
The trunk is thicker, the leaves longer and more lax, and the flower stalks 2 or 3 times as long as broad.

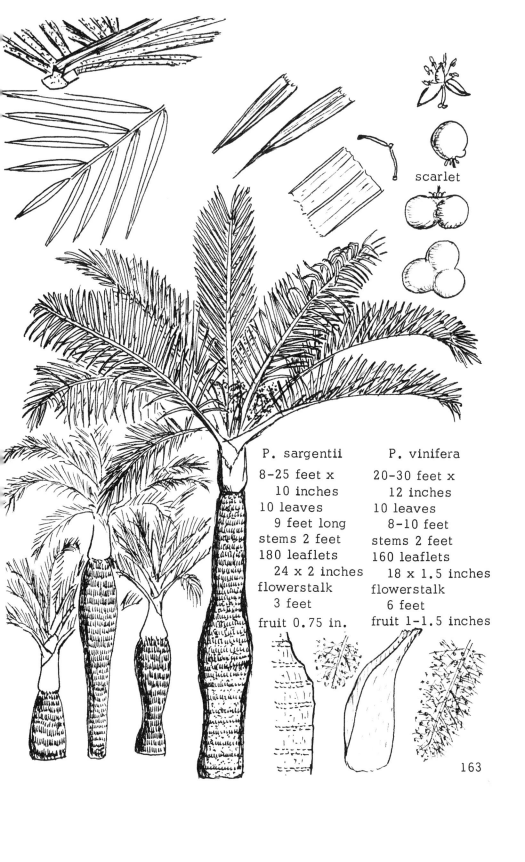

scarlet

P. sargentii

8-25 feet x
  10 inches
10 leaves
  9 feet long
stems 2 feet
180 leaflets
  24 x 2 inches
flowerstalk
  3 feet
fruit 0.75 in.

P. vinifera

20-30 feet x
  12 inches
10 leaves
  8-10 feet
stems 2 feet
160 leaflets
  18 x 1.5 inches
flowerstalk
  6 feet
fruit 1-1.5 inches

163

CHRYSALIDOCARPUS

About 20 species comprise this genus, all native to the island of Madagascar. Those that have been tried here have done superlatively well.

Trunks are multiple in all 3 species, but one has a variety with a solitary trunk. In all of them, the appearance of the trunk varies with age; in young trees the trunk is smooth and green, with the ring-scars slightly raised and dull white or light brown; in older trees the trunk is gray. The crownshaft in younger trees is extended, as the ring-scars are 4 to 6 inches apart, preventing the trunk from being compact. As the growth rate slows, the crown shortens.

The leafstem bases are prominently ridged below the leafstem. The sheath is usually split half way or more on the other side of the trunk. Leafstems are twisted on some leaves, not on all. The leaflets, held in a V, are green on both sides, ribbed on the margins, with unequal tips that are sharp but split as they die back. Reins are not common in this genus.

CHRYSALIDOCARPUS MADAGASCARIENSIS
Malagasy Palm

Several trunks (up to 6) on swollen bases carry the crowns of leaves in vertical rows of 3. The leaflets are many ranked, in groups of 3 or 4, held in a V, and lax at the midpoint. This species is fairly common, and deserves to be more popular.

C. MADAGASCARIENSIS VAR. LUCUBENSIS
Lucuba Palm

Identical to the above, but with only one trunk. An attractive palm, but not common here.

20-25 feet x 3 inches
10-12 leaves 10 feet long
stems 4-6 inches
240 leaflets 20 x 1 inch
flowerstalk 4 feet
fruit 0.5 inch, black

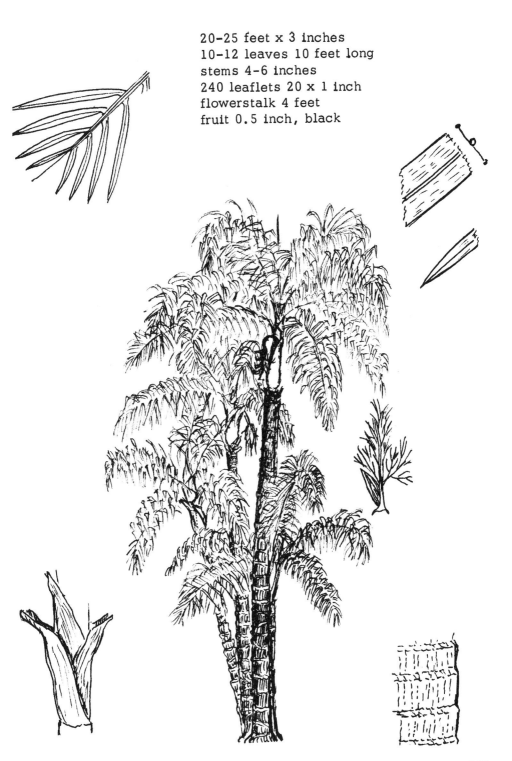

CHRYSALIDOCARPUS LUTESCENS

Yellow Butterfly Palm

This species is an old Florida favorite. It is often called the Areca Palm, an unfortunate misnomer, as the true Areca is solitary, tall, and very rare here.

The trunks are numerous, clumping, thin, green, and ringed, resembling bamboo. The leafstems and midribs are yellow. The leaflets are bright green, but in full sunlight they can be yellow green. They are lax only near the tip, are in one plane, and are held in a narrow V. One bract surrounds the flower stalk, and soon is shed; another persists at the base of the stalk.

CHRYSALIDOCARPUS CABADAE   Cabada Palm

A relative newcomer amongst us, the Cabada came to this area from Cuba, and is not known in its presumed land of origin, which must be Madagascar. As many as 14 trunks occur, each on a swollen base. The leaves are in vertical rows of three when seen from below. The leaflets are in one plane, held in a wide V, and lax near the tip. The species grows very fast, and it may be expected to become one of our best palms.

Ganoderma is known to have killed specimens of the Yellow Butterfly Palm, and it must be expected that the other species in the genus are also susceptible.

25 feet x 3-5 inches
6-8 leaves 8 feet
stems 2 feet
80-120 leaflets
    20 x 1.5 inches
flowerstalk 3 feet
fruit 1 inch, yellow

20-30 foot x 5 inches
6-10 leaves 10-12 feet
stems 2-4 feet
120 leaflets 24 x 2 in.
flowerstalk 5 feet
fruit 0.5 inch, red

PINNATE LEAF PALMS

REDUPLICATE

NO SPINES

NO CROWNSHAFT

ATTALEA, MAXIMILIANA, ORBIGNYA, SCHEELEA
THE SOUTH AMERICAN OIL PALMS

These four genera are quite similar in appearance, and few botanists, if any, dare to classify them without careful regard to the floral parts. Several species have been tried here in South Florida, with reasonable success, but the Oil Palms are still uncommon. Their size prevents their use on small lots.

The trunk is hidden in the youth of the tree by the leaves, and later by the persistent leafbases. In age, the trunk is evident; it is thick, light brown, and the surface is marked with smooth, undulating ring-scars of exceptional width. There is no crownshaft.

The leafstems are remarkably long, and ascend close to the trunk. The leafstem bases produce long, round, light gray fibers that do not form sharp projections as they decay. The leaflets are long, dark green, and may be once or several ranked. The margins are only slightly ribbed, and the tips are sharp pointed.

Each flower stalk is surmounted by a long, narrow spathe with an extremely long point. Male and female flowers are borne on different stalks. The genera may be segregated by study of the male flowers.

Attalea (40 species in S. America); petals flattened, angular, not curved at the tip.

Maximiliana (10 species in S. America and the West Indies); petals minute.

Orbignya (25 species in S. America); petals shaped like a boat, curved at the top; anthers spiralled.

Scheelea (40 species in Mexico, Central and South America, the West Indies); petals slender, like exclamation points, longer than the unspiralled anthers.

40-70 feet x 2 feet
50-80 leaves
  30-40 feet long
400 (?) leaflets
  2 feet x 1-3
  inches
fruit 1-4 inches,
  green to brown,
  smooth, hard

ELAEIS

Two species comprise the genus Elaeis. The African
Oil Palm is of great economic importance, as the oil,
extracted from the fruit, is widely used in soaps, for
lighting, and in cooking. It can be grown in our area
without difficulty, but it is a large palm, and enough
space must be allowed.

ELAEIS GUINEENSIS   African Oil Palm
The trunk is solitary, but sometimes a seed sprouts
beside the parent tree, and gives the impression of a
multiple stem. The trunk is straight, with irregular
bulging usually at middle height. Ring-scars are wide
and raised, but do not encircle the tree. Some of the
old leafstem bases, reduced to thick triangular plates,
persist at the base or above it.

The leafstems, from the trunk to the leaflet rows,
produce thick threads of fiber; these wear away, but
the tough basal portion remains as jagged projections.
In addition to this, the leaflets nearest to the base of
the leaf die back, but their sturdy midribs remain as
imitation spines, each set on a rounded leaflet base.
The leaves die as they descend to the horizontal, and
the tree has a characteristic umbrella silhouette. The
leaflets are widely three ranked, and abruptly and obliquely sharp pointed.

The two bracts are papery and soon fall. Each tree
bears flowers of both sexes, but on separate flower
stalks. The male flowers appear in thick, finger·like
structures. The fruit grows in short, dense clusters
(to 300 fruit) whose color differs with the variety. The
seeds have 3 pores near the tip end. A tree bears at
4 to 5 years, a new leaf developes every two weeks,
lasting for 3 1/2 to 4 years. A male flower stalk may
have as many as 140,000 flowers, a female as many
as 5,000, and it takes 5 to 6 months for the fruit to
become fully ripened.

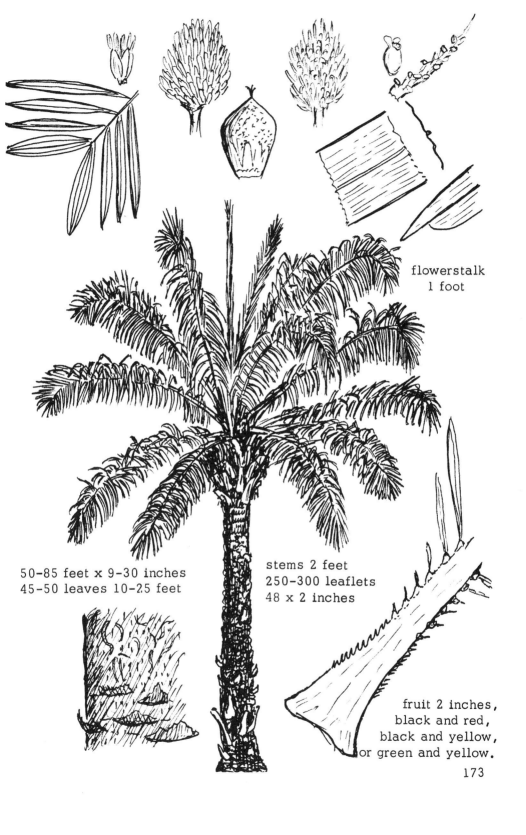

flowerstalk
1 foot

50-85 feet x 9-30 inches
45-50 leaves 10-25 feet

stems 2 feet
250-300 leaflets
48 x 2 inches

fruit 2 inches,
black and red,
black and yellow,
or green and yellow.

173

BUTIA

The Jelly Palm is one of 13 members of the genus Butia, or one of the 49 members of the genus Syagrus. It is from Brazil, and has been used as an ornamental in North Florida, where it seems to do better than it does south of Lake Okeechobee. It is reputed to be hardy to North Carolina. It hybridizes easily with the other Syagrus species. It is drought resistant, once it has become established. This is another species of palm that is subject to the attacks of Ganoderma.

BUTIA CAPITATA   Jelly Palm
The trunk is dark brown, the incomplete ring-scars sharply ridged. Large, thick, gray leafbases persist irregularly around the trunk, and are most numerous near the crown. There is no crownshaft.

The broadly based leafstems produce a row of thick curly hair on each edge; this breaks down into sharply pointed projections that often appear to be a series of teeth. The leaves are stiff, sharply ascending at the trunk, then curled in a tight arch. The leaflets are a blue green, in a plane, and held in a pronounced V. The tips are sharply pointed, often split and blunted with age.

The spathe is large and woody, and smooth on the back. The once branched stalk supports flowers that may be red, yellow, or a shade of purple. The females develope at the base of the branches, the males near the tip. The fruit is edible, and used for jelly or wine.

Butia bonnetii is now considered to be an immature form of B. capitata, rather than a separate species.

5-20 feet x 1.5 feet
45-50 leaves 4-6 feet long
stems 4 feet long
140 leaflets 30 x 1 inch
flowerstalk 30 inches
fruit 1 inch, yellow to orange

175

SYAGRUS

The genus Syagrus has northern South America as its home, centering on Brazil. The number of species in the genus may be 34, according to one system of classification, or 49, according to another that lumps such palms as Butia, Arecastrum, and Arikuryroba with the 34 others. One of the arguments for the latter scheme is that they all hybridize under the right conditions. Few of the Syagrus species (by the first and older plan) are well known in South Florida, and most of these are very similar in appearance to the Queen Palm, Arecastrum romanzoffianum. Syagrus coronata, however, is markedly different in several important aspects.

SYAGRUS CORONATA   Licury Palm

The trunk below the crown is completely obscured by old leafstem bases, which are arranged in vertical or in spiralled rows, each 5 bases thick.

The strips of fiber on the sides of the leafstems wear away to tough cores, forming thin, flat, square-tipped projections. The leaves are held stiffly upright. The leaflets are stiff, dark green, and many ranked, with sharply pointed tips. They are attached in groups of 2 to 4 near the midpoint of the leaf.

The spathe is large, woody, and long lasting. Male and female flowers grow on the same stalk.

30 feet x 10 inches thick
25 leaves 10 feet long
stems 2 feet
240 leaflets 18 x 1.5 inch
flowerstalk 3 feet
fruit 1 inch, orange yellow

SYAGRUS   (continued)

A hybrid between Arecastrum and Butia, known only
from Central and South Florida, has become a popular
landscape palm in the area immediately south of Lake
Okeechobee. It combines the outstanding features of
its parents. Like them, it is probably susceptible to
Ganoderma. The first specimen to be scientifically
studied and named came from Fairchild Tropical Garden,
but the palm was not originated there.

SYAGRUS X FAIRCHILDENSIS
The solitary trunk is largely covered with leafstem
bases, 8 inches wide and several feet long, with gray
surfaces. There is no crownshaft.

The leafstems produce a large amount of fiber at the
trunk, and some, but not much, toward the leaflets.
There are no sharp projections along the edges of the
leafstems, as in Butia. The leaflets are slightly two
ranked, of a moderate green on both sides, and not as
stiff as those of Butia nor as lax as in Arecastrum.
They are held in a slight V. The midribs are raised on
the upper surface, and smooth on the underside.

The spathe is very long, moderately woody, and does
not have the deep groves on the back as in Arecastrum.

15-30 feet x 15 inches
20 leaves 15 feet long
stems 3 feet

180 leaflets 30 x 1 inch
flowerstalk 6 feet
fruit 1 inch, yellow
to orange

179

NEODYPSIS

Madagascar, the large island on Africa's east coast, has about 15 species of Neodypsis. Only one of these has been disseminated, and that sparingly, in South Florida. Given enough good soil, it flourishes, but in thin, poor soil it survives but does not thrive. It will respond well to a liberal use of fertilizer.

NEODYPSIS DECARYI   Triangle Palm

Trunks of this species are solitary, short, sturdy and dark brown, with thin gray ring-scars raised above the surface. Near the crown the trunk is usually studded with assorted remnants of old, dead leafbases.

The leafbases form a distinctive crown of 3 vertical rows. Younger leafbases are covered with a red wool that wears away. The leafstems are long, very straight and stiff until near the tip, where they become strongly down curved. The one-planed leaflets are very stiff and sharp pointed, and are held in a narrow V. Both leafstems and leaflets are a light gray green. Reins are exceptionally long and thick in this species.

The flower stalks grow among the leaves. Two flat bracts surround the budding stalk; one soon falls, but the other persists. The stalk divides into branches and then into branchlets. Male and female flowers, small and yellow, occur separately on the same branchlets.

flowerstalk 5 feet
fruit 1 inch, yellow
green

9-18 feet x 12-16 inches
20 leaves 8-10 feet long
stems 12 inches
100-190 leaflets
30 x 2 inches

181

ARECASTRUM (SYAGRUS)

The Queen Palm is alone in the genus Arecastrum, or it is one of many palms in the genus Syagrus. There seem to be several varieties, based on the width of the trunk, the length of the leaflets, and the size of the fruit. The tree is encountered everywhere in our area, and it has been an important ornamental here for many years. Where space is available, this species has no disqualifying traits, and it thrives under poor care and in a wide range of soils. Some individuals have fallen victims to the parasitic fungus, Ganoderma.

ARECASTRUM ROMANZOFFIANUM   Queen Palm

The solitary trunk is erect, light gray, and slightly and irregularly bulging. The surface is smooth but for a slight roughness at the ring-scars. Rarely, one or several old leafstem bases will project from the trunk as tough, gray, rectangular plates. The fibers along the leafstems are soft, and do not form sharp points.

The leafstem bases spread widely, but the lowest of them have no live tissue clasping the trunk, although the ring-scars they leave are complete. The leaves are few and arched, with leaflets that are many ranked, in groups of 2 to 7 along the stem. They bend sharply at or near the midpoint. Faint auxiliary ribs mark the upper side of the leaflet. The leaflet tips are sharply pointed, but die back and become blunt.

The spathe that protects the flower stalk is slender, woody, and very long, with deep parallel folding on the outer surface. The stalk branches once, and carries the flowers of both sexes. Female flowers are alone at the base, while those in the central portion are in triads with two males each, and the tips of the branches are given over completely to males.

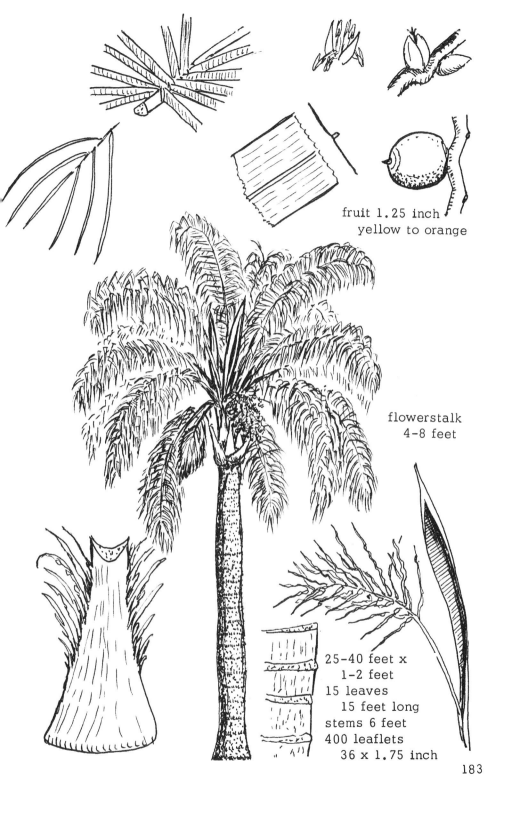

fruit 1.25 inch
yellow to orange

flowerstalk
4-8 feet

25-40 feet x
1-2 feet
15 leaves
15 feet long
stems 6 feet
400 leaflets
36 x 1.75 inch

183

COCOS

The Coconut Palm is the only species in its genus. From its point of origin, probably in southeast Asia, it has been spread by mankind to all tropical coasts. It is, beyond a doubt, the palm species with the greatest number of individuals on the planet. Centuries of cultivation have given us possibly as many as 80 named varieties. Lethal yellowing, a disease whose nature is still not understood, appears to be fatal to most of these; apparently, only the yellow strain of the Malay Golden, or Dwarf, Coconut, is known to be immune.

COCOS NUCIFERA   Coconut Palm
The trunk is solitary; twinned trunks are rare, while three stems from one nut are not unknown. In any case, the base is swollen, and the trunk curving. The surface of the trunk is a light gray brown, clean but rough with prominent, crescent shaped, complete ring-scars. The fiber matting at the base of the leafstems is extraordinarily well developed, strongly resembling cloth, and sometimes used as such.

The broad leafbases do not encircle the trunk, and there is no crownshaft. The leafstems twist only to a slight degree. Leaflets are flat, in a plane, smooth of margin, pointed of tip, and fairly lax.

The flower stalks have two bracts; the first one, the shortest, persists on the base of the stalk; the second becomes the large, pointed, woody "boat" that remains a part of the tree until the last of the fruit ripens and the stalk falls. The stalk has a few simple branches, a very few large female flowers near the base, and a large number of males scattered about. The fruit takes 9 to 12 months to ripen after the flowers open.

60-80 feet x 16-24 inches
28-30 leaves 15-19 feet long
stems 3-4 feet
150-180 leaflets 36
36 x 1.5 inches

fruit
1 foot,
green
yellow
or
brown

flowerstalk
3-4 feet

185

GAUSSIA

The islands of Puerto Rico and Cuba have given us
the two Gaussia Palms. They grow on limestone rock
in their native lands, usually on cliffsides to which
they cling with long, exposed roots. While both grow
well in South Florida, neither has received widespread
acceptance, probably because of their undernourished
aspect. As young plants, they require partial shade,
but are able to stand full sunlight when mature.

The solitary trunks are light brown and banded with
wide ring-scars in young trees, smooth and gray when
mature. The crownshaft is poorly formed, and usually
obscured by persistent dead leafbases, some of which
may bear long leaflet-less stems. The trunks taper
more than those of any other palm in our area.

The leaves are few and relatively short. The many
ranked leaflets are numerous, flat, narrow, and taper
to a broad, sharp point. They are deciduous, falling
one by one, instead of holding on until the leaf falls.
The upper surface is smooth, and the midrib is raised
on the underside. Large callouses form at the point of
attachment. There are no reins, and no marginal ribs.

The very long flower stalks develope in the crown of
leaves, and persist after the leaves below them fall to
the ground. The stalks are twice branched. Flower
buds are in chains of 3 to 5, the lowest one female.

GAUSSIA ATTENUATA   Puerto Rican Gaussia
The leaflets of this species have secondary ribs near
the margins.

GAUSSIA PRINCEPS   Sierra Palm
The leaflets of the Sierra Palm do not have secondary
ribs. The callous at the point of attachment is larger
than in the above species.

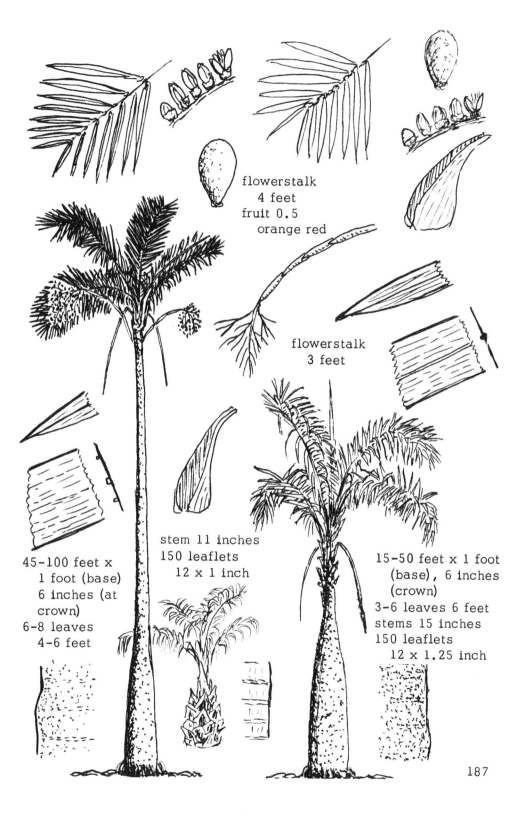

flowerstalk
4 feet
fruit 0.5
orange red

flowerstalk
3 feet

stem 11 inches
150 leaflets
12 x 1 inch

45-100 feet x
1 foot (base)
6 inches (at
crown)
6-8 leaves
4-6 feet

15-50 feet x 1 foot
(base), 6 inches
(crown)
3-6 leaves 6 feet
stems 15 inches
150 leaflets
12 x 1.25 inch

187

HETEROSPATHE

Eighteen or more species of palms from the Philippine Islands, New Guinea, and Indonesia make up the genus. Only one species has been accepted in South Florida, and is still rare here; others are being tried.

HETEROSPATHE ELATA

Young trees have a smooth brown surface with ring-scars of yellow brown about an inch wide; older trees wear to a mousey gray surface, and may have closely spaced vertical fissures. The trunks are solitary and tapering, the often swollen base nearly twice as thick as the top of the tree. There is no crownshaft, as the leafbases do not form sheaths, but break up at the sides into masses of yellow fiber.

The leaves are stiffly arched. The leafstems twist more than do those of most other palms, the plane of leaflets near the base is horizontal, that of those at the tip is vertical. The leaflets are in a plane, with ribbed margins and sharp tips that fray and split. The midrib is raised on the upper surface, and there are one or two sets of secondary ribs on the underside. New leaves may be a light red brown. Reins do occur, but not frequently.

The flower stalks are among the lower leaves, but survive them to hang below the crown. Two bracts, a spathe and a thin strap, fall before the stalk is fully grown. The stalk is short and heavy, and divides into branches and branchlets. The flowers are small and white, two males to each female, spiralling around the branchlets.

30-45 feet x 7 inches
10-16 leaves 5-10 feet long
stems 27 inches
130 leaflets 2-3 feet x
   1.5 inches
flowerstalk 4 feet
fruit 0.5 inch, white to red

OPSIANDRA

The only species of this genus is from Guatemala and neighboring countries. The palm appears to like South Florida growing conditions, but requires partial shade to be at its best. It tends to blow down rather easily in hurricanes.

OPSIANDRA MAYA   Maya Palm

The solitary trunk is a smooth light brown, the ring-scars stepped. That part of the trunk below the crown is green, with brown ring-scars. The trunk is swollen at the base, and fat horizontal roots are visible above ground. The crownshaft is poorly formed, as the ring-scars are so far apart (3-5 inches), and the leafstem bases are so deeply notched in the back. A few old leafbases usually depend below the crown.

The leaves are ascending, falling while still above the horizontal. The leaflets are many ranked, flat and smooth on the upper surface, with the midrib and one or two sets of secondary ribs raised above the surface on the underside. The leaflet margins are not ribbed, and the tips are sharply pointed. The leaflets are deciduous, shedding from the leafstem, and the leafstem often breaks free from the leafstem base. There are no reins on the leaves of this species.

The flower stalks develope far down the trunk, well below the crown, appearing as buds at several of the ring-scars. Five tubular bracts cover the stalk that divides only once, into branches; these bear the small male and female flowers and the white, then red, fruit. The stalks ripen their fruit serially, from the bottom, and it is often possible to observe buds, flowers, the green fruit, and the ripe fruit, all at the same time.

20-60 feet x 8 inches (base), 5 inches (crown)
5-7 leaves 9 feet long on 4 foot stems
160 leaflets 2 feet x 2 inches
flowerstalk 3 feet
fruit 0.75 inch, white becoming red

191

HOWEIA

The Lord Howe Islands, 600 miles east of Australia, are the only home of the Howeia Palms. (Note that in the nursery trade, they are often called Kentias, but this name was formerly given to them in error). The two attractive species are well known in this country, chiefly as potted plants. Out of doors in South Florida they do well in partial shade, but they are slow.

The solitary trunks are swollen at the base. At the crown the trunk is green, becoming gray a few feet on down. The ring-scars are undulating, and are slightly raised above the smooth surface. There is no crown-shaft. The leafstem bases break down into fiber.

The leaves are very numerous. The long leafstems appear to arch reluctantly away from the trunk. The leaflets are in a plane, and are dark green above and a bit lighter beneath. They have pleated folds, ribbed margins, and pointed tips that fray as they die back.

The flowers appear on a spike or on several spikes, with one papery bract. Two male flowers grow beside one female flower, in pits in the fleshy stalk.

HOWEIA BELMOREANA   Belmore Sentry Palm
Of the two species, this is the shorter, with fewer, more ascending leaves. The leaflets are held in a V. The pleats on the leaflets are less noticeable. One spike bears the flowers and the beak-tipped fruit.

HOWEIA FORSTERIANA   Forster Sentry Palm
This species has more leaves, and the leafstems are more lax. The leaflets are horizontal, at the leafstem, and then curve downward. The pleats in the leaflets are prominent. Spikes, 3 to 8, bear rounded fruit.

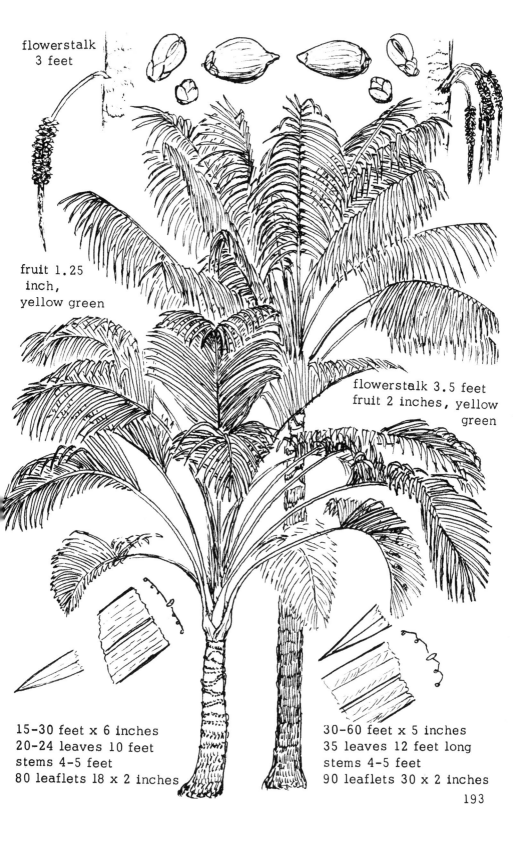

flowerstalk
3 feet

fruit 1.25
inch,
yellow green

flowerstalk 3.5 feet
fruit 2 inches, yellow
green

15-30 feet x 6 inches
20-24 leaves 10 feet
stems 4-5 feet
80 leaflets 18 x 2 inches

30-60 feet x 5 inches
35 leaves 12 feet long
stems 4-5 feet
90 leaflets 30 x 2 inches

ARIKURYROBA

The Arikury Palm, from Brazil, is one of three palms in its genus, or it may be another Syagrus. It is known to hybridize with Syagrus coronata. It does best in the full sunlight, and will not succeed in deep shade. A young plant makes an attractive potted specimen, when the trunk has not yet appeared. This is another of the species that can be a host to Ganoderma.

ARIKURYROBA SCHIZOPHYLLA   Arikury Palm

The trunk is solitary, erect, short, moderately thick, and a dark brown. The old leafstem bases are spiralled around the trunk, sometimes reduced to small protuberances, sometimes retaining oblong plates of decaying stem tissue. Weak fiber matting, in small quantities, is produced among the leafstem bases.

The purple brown leafstems are thin at the basal end, light green and even thinner at the leaf end. Rows of fiber threads along the leafstem margins break down to sharp projections that point upward. The leaves crowd together at the crown, and are short, with few leaflets. These leaflets are the same light green on both sides, and are moderately lax, with unribbed margins and tips with an abrupt point. The leaflets are in one plane.

The flower stalk divides once, into simple branches. The female flowers are grouped at the lower portion of the branches, with the males scattered to the top. The woody bract is long, on a narrow stalk. The fruit is edible, but is rather insipidly sweet.

9 feet x
6-8 inches
25-30 leaves
6 feet long
80 leaflets
24 x 1.5 inch

flowerstalk 3 feet
fruit 1 inch, orange

POLYANDROCOCOS

The Buri Palm is not well known as yet in this region, but it has qualities that should make it popular, when available. It is from Brazil, and is the only species in its genus.

POLYANDROCOCOS CAUDESCENS   Buri Palm

The trunk is straight, solitary, and light brown, very nearly stepped by the incomplete ring-scars. Younger trees often have the trunk completely hidden by broad, ridged, light brown leafstem bases. Threads of yellow fiber are produced along the sides of the leafstems.

The unarmed leafstems are deep green from the base to the tip of the leaf. They ascend steeply, then arch outward. The leaflets are flat, stiff, and in one plane, dark green and glossy above, with silver hairs on the under side. The leaflet tips are sharply pointed and a bit oblique.

The spathe is woody and persistent. Flower stalks, appearing in the crown, are unbranched, and carry the flowers of both sexes. The males blossom first, hiding the females with stamens of a dull rose. When they fall they reveal the light orange female flowers.

The name, Buri, is from the language of one of the native tribes. Another Buri Palm exists, the completely dissimilar Corypha elata, and its common name is taken from a native dialect in India.

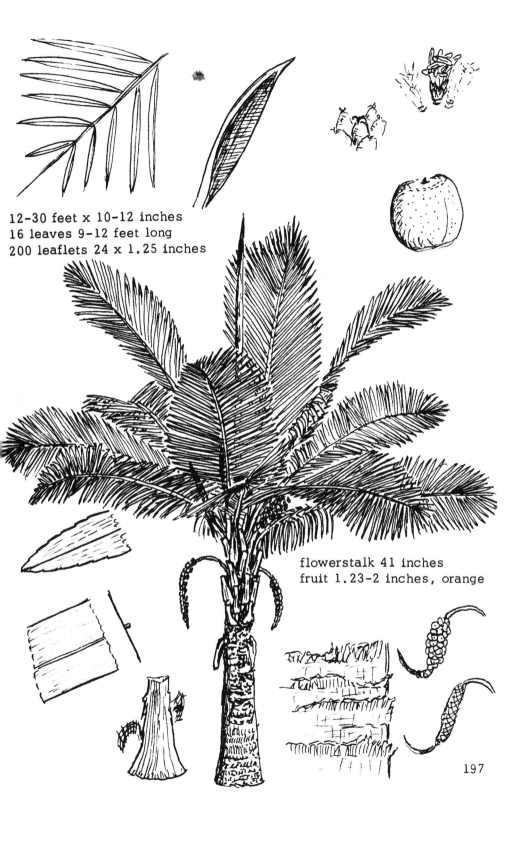

12-30 feet x 10-12 inches
16 leaves 9-12 feet long
200 leaflets 24 x 1.25 inches

flowerstalk 41 inches
fruit 1.23-2 inches, orange

197

SYNECHANTHUS

Six species of this genus grow in deep woodlands in Central and northern South America. Only one can be found in South Florida gardens. It requires water in greater amounts than our rainfall provides.

SYNECHANTHUS FIBROSUS

The rather slender, solitary trunk is erect, a glossy green, the complete ring-scars brown. Several papery leafstem bases usually adhere below the crown, but there is no true crownshaft.

The leafstems are ascending, holding the leaves above the horizontal, and are not twisted. The leaves are a light green on both sides. The leaflets are in a plane, thin and flexible, some with secondary ribs, and occurring interruptedly along the leafstem. The terminal leaflets on each side have 5 to 9 ribs. Tips are sharply pointed, and margins are not ribbed.

The flower stalk developes among the leaves, with 2 tubular bracts. Both male and female flowers appear along the twice-branched stalk.

Palms of the genus Synechanthus were once thought to be Chamaedoreas, before it was known that the male and female flowers occur on the same flower stalk in this genus, and on different trees in Chamaedoreas.

10-15 feet x 2-3 inches
13 leaves 5 feet long on 18 inch stems
30-40 leaflets 16 x 1.5 inches

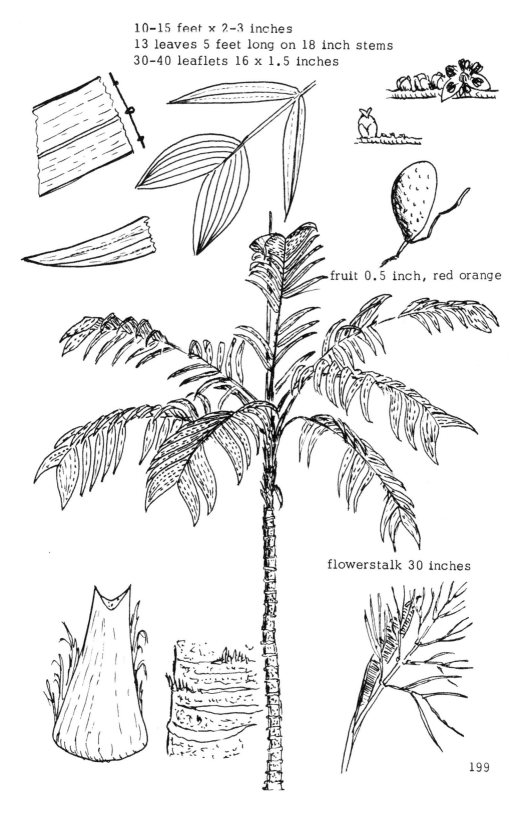

fruit 0.5 inch, red orange

flowerstalk 30 inches

PINANGA

India, the Celebes Islands, and Malaysia have 115
or more species of Pinangas. Many of them have been
tried here, but most of them have proved to be too cold
tender and too intolerant of our poor, alkaline soils.
Some of them have been brought in under wrong names,
and it is possible that only the one species is now in
our area. It is a small, shade loving, slow growing
palm, spreading in clumps to 20 feet across.

PINANGA KUHLII

The trunks are multiple, slender, green, and smooth,
with light brown ring-scars. The ragged crownshaft is
much wider than the trunk.

The leafstems are thin, and partly covered with tiny
brown scales. The leaflets are in a plane and light
green. They are attached to the leafstem in groups of
2 to 10, nearly opposite one another. Leaflet margins
are not ribbed. Leaflet tips curve forward to give one
long, thinly pointed tip to most groups of leaflets, and
a broad, jagged tip to the terminal leaflet. There are
no reins, and the leafstems are not twisted. The new
growth is pink, soon turning light green.

One bract encloses the developing flower stalk, and
it falls before the flowers mature. The stalk has from
6 to 8 short, simple branches.

5-20 feet x 2 inches
5-6 leaves 3-5 feet long
stems 16 inches

leaflet number variable

flower stalk 12 inches
fruit 0.5 inch, dark red

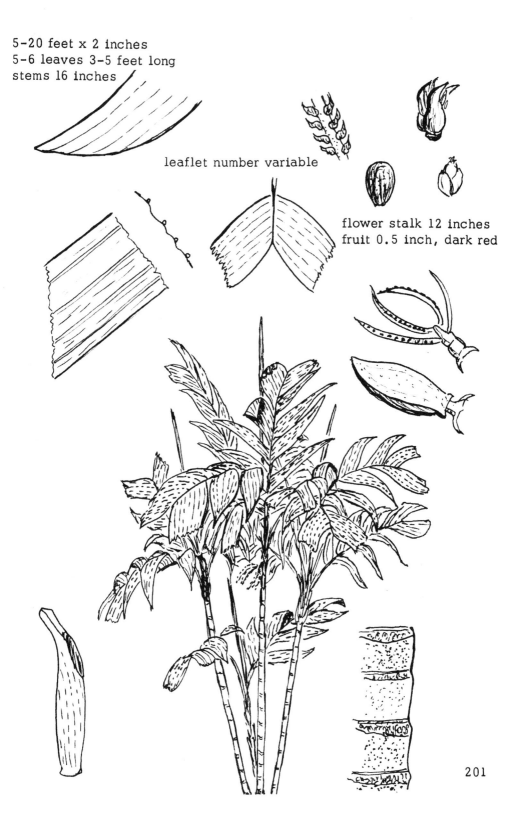

GEONOMA

Some 150 species of Geonoma have been described,
from shaded forests in Central America, northern South
America, and the islands of the Caribbean. How many
of these have been introduced into the United States
is a presently unsettled point. At least three former
species have been combined recently, G. oxycarpa
and G. binervia being joined to G. interrupta.

GEONOMA INTERRUPTA

The trunks are solitary and variable, some of them
reaching 23 feet, others only 4, with thicknesses from
1 to 5 inches. In South Florida, a height of 6 feet with
a thickness of 3 inches would probably be a good tree,
12 years after the palm was planted, as they are slow.
The surface of the trunk is a pale, warm brown, smooth
but for the slightly raised gray ring-scars spaced 1/2
to 1 1/2 inches apart. There is no crownshaft, as the
leafbases break down into thin strips of fibrous matter.
Old leafbases persist below the crown, often in a sad
state of decay.

The leaves are light green on both sides, somewhat
glossy above, and flat. The leaflets are in groups, a
portion of bare leafstem between them, often with 30
to 80 midribs divided among 10 to 30 groups on each
side. The groups appear to be random in composition
and distribution, and not evenly numbered and spaced
as in Pinanga. There are no reins.

The flower stalk is short, with one flat, heart shaped
outer bract splitting to reveal a second, similar bract.
The stalk may branch once, twice, or thrice. Flowers
of both sexes develope in pits, two males beside one
female.

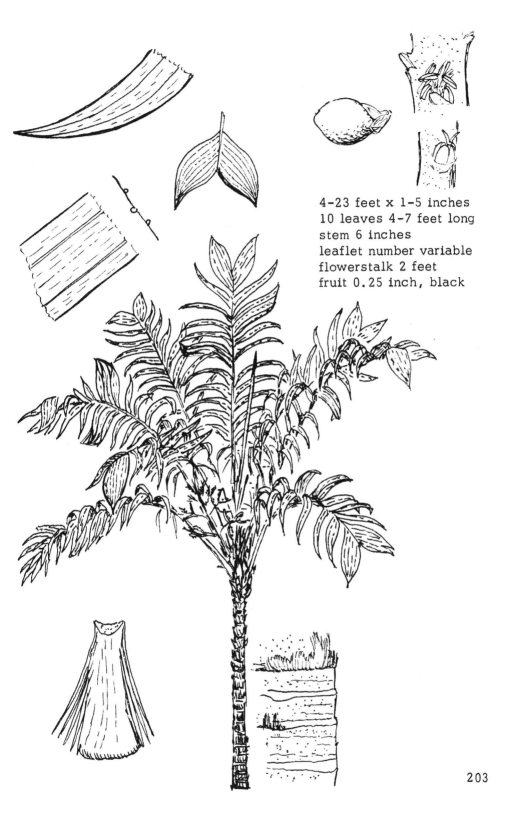

4-23 feet x 1-5 inches
10 leaves 4-7 feet long
stem 6 inches
leaflet number variable
flowerstalk 2 feet
fruit 0.25 inch, black

203

CHAMAEDOREA

From the densely shaded forests of southern Mexico through Venezuela and on into Peru, there are at least 100 species of Chamaedorea. Of this number, quite a few have found their way into conservatories, gardens, and homes in the United States, some with names that are not scientifically established. Until the genus is reviewed, the names used herein should be considered to be conditional, subject to later correction. Another problem in Chamaedoreas is the amount of hybridization that can occur between closely related species; again, the answers may be forthcoming, but they are not available now.

Many species have but a solitary trunk, others have several; a few are vine-like climbers; some have no trunk at all. Where trunks are present, they are very thin, 2 inches thick at the most, less than half of that as an average. They are green and smooth, with gray ring-scars, resembling the stems of slender bamboo. The crownshafts are poor, as the leafstem bases are deeply notched and the ring-scars far apart. Leaves are pinnately veined, with the leaflets separate from one another except for the terminal pair -- but two species have completely undivided leaves. Leaflets are usually deciduous.

The flower stalks grow among the lower leaves, but survive them. Bracts number from 3 to 7, and stalks may be unbranched, or branched once or twice. Male and female flowers appear on different plants.

A KEY TO THE COMMON CHAMAEDOREAS

Trunk solitary, erect
  Leaflets undivided
    Bright green leaf 2'. . . . . . . C. ernesti-angusti
    Dark green leaf 10" . . . . C. metallica

  Leaflets divided
    Leaflets in several planes . . . . . . C. glaucifolia
    Leaflets in one plane
      Trunk 2" thick . . . . C. tepejilote
      Trunk 1" thick or less
        Leaflets under 2" wide . . . . . . C. elegans
        Leaflets over 2" wide
          Leaves to 5', leaflets deciduous . C. arenbergiana
          Leaves to 3', leaflets not deciduous
            Aerial roots; 30" flower stalk . .C. concolor
            No a. roots; 15" flower stalk . C. oblongata

Trunk solitary, sprawling, vine like. . . . C. elatior

Trunks multiple, over 3' tall
  Leaflets 3/4" wide . . . . C. seifrizii
  Leaflets 1-2" wide
    Leaves 18-20", fruit black . . . . . C. erumpens
    Leaves 24-30", fruit red . . . . . C. microspadix

Trunkless, or trunk less than 1' tall
  Leaves 3', flower stalk 4'. . . . . . . C. radicalis
  Leaves 2', flower stalk 2' . . . . C. cataractarum

Of the Chamaedoreas now in use, the best and most
common are C. seifrizii, C. elegans, C. erumpens,
and C. cataractarum.

205

CHAMAEDOREA   (continued)

C. ERNESTI-ANGUSTI

Trunk 4 feet x 0.75 inch,
some aerial roots. Leaves
3-9, not divided, dull medium green, ribs 15 inches.
Flowerstalks 2 feet; male
green, branched once, the
female orange, a spike.
Both flowers orange. Fruit
0.5 inch.

C. METALLICA

Trunk to 4 feet x 0.5
inch, some aerial roots.
Leaves 12-16, 10 inches,
undivided, dark green,
metallic, glossy. Flowerstalks 18 inches; male with
10-12 branches, female a
spike. Fruit 0.5 inch,
black.

C. GLAUCIFOLIA

Trunk to 20 feet x 1 inch.
Leaves 6-8, 4-8 feet, gray
green. Leaflets 120, 12-
15 inches, 0.5 inch wide,
midrib off center; several
ranked, spaced unequally;
distinct callous at base.
Flowerstalks once branched;
male green, female red.
Fruit green, 0.25 inch.

CHAMAEDOREA (continued)

C. TEPEJILOTE
Trunk to 12 feet x 2 inches,
aerial roots. Leaves 507, to
5 feet, dark green. Leaflets
32-48, 20 x 1.5-2 inches,
deciduous, 6 secondary ribs
on upper side. Flower stalk
2 feet, orange, once branched.
Fruit green to black. 0.5 inch.

C. ELEGANS
Trunk to 10 feet x 1 inch.
Leaves 5-15, 15-36 inches,
medium green both sides.
Leaflets 20-40, 6-9 inches x
0.75-1 inch, margins not ribbed.
Flowerstalks 6-36 inches,
branched twice, orange. Fruit
black, 0.2 inch. (This species
is often sold as Neanthe bella.)

C. ARENBERGIANA
Trunk to 9 feet x 1 inch.
Leaves 6, 5 feet, dull dark green.
Leaflets 16-30, 8-12 inches x
3-7 inches, with 5-15 ribs each.
Flowerstalks 8-12 inches, male
once branched, female a spike
like an ear of corn, both orange.
Fruit black, 0.3 inch.

C. CONCOLOR

Trunk to 8 feet x 0.75 inch, some aerial roots. Leaves 4-5, 30 inches, bright green, shiny. Leaflets 10-14, 10 x 3 inches, margins ribbed. Terminal leaflets large, 5-6 ribs. Leaflets deciduous. Flowerstalk 1-2 feet, orange, once branched. Fruit red, 0.3 inch.

C. OBLONGATA

Trunk to 9 feet x 0.5 inch, clean. Leaves 5-8, 3 feet, shiny light green. Leaflets 10-16, 9 x 3-4 inches, margins ribbed on underside. Terminal leaflets small, 3-5 ribs. Flowerstalk once or twice branched, orange. Fruit dark green, 0.3 inch.

C. ELATIOR

Trunk vine like, variable in length, 1 inch wide. Leaves 4-12, 6-8 inches, dark green both sides, leaflets about 30, 24 x 1 inch, many small pleats, margin not ribbed. Flowerstalk orange, once branched. Fruit not observed.

CHAMAEDOREA (continued)

C. SEIFRIZII
Trunks to 12 feet x 0.75 inch. Leaves 6-9, 2 feet, dull dark green. Leaflets 24-36, 8 x 0.75 inch, margins ribbed. Terminal leaflet 4-5 ribs. Flowerstalk 6-12 inches, branched once, orange. Fruit green to black, 0.25 inch.

C. ERUMPENS
Trunks to 12 feet x 0.5 inch. Leaves 6-8, dark glossy green both sides. Two forms: A, leaflets 32-40 8 x 1.5 inch; B, leaflets 20-24, 8 x 2-3 inches. Flowerstalk 6-12 inches, once branched, orange. Fruit black, 0.25 inch.

C. MICROSPADIX
Trunks to 10 feet x 0.5 inch. Leaves 4-8, 24-30 inches, dull dark green both sides. Leaflets 16-30, 6 to 10 x 1-2 inches, smooth below, margins ribbed above. Terminal leaflets broad, 4-5 ribs. Flowerstalk 8-24 inch branched once, yellow. Fruit orange to red. 0.3 inch.

CHAMAEDOREA (continued)

C. RADICALIS
   Trunkless. Leaves 6-8,
3 feet, dark green on both
sides. Leaflets 36-40, 14 x
1 inch, margins not ribbed,
no secondary ribs, terminal
leaflet large. Flowerstalk
54 inches, once branched,
orange. Fruit orange,
0.4 inch.

C. CATARACTARUM
   Trunkless. Leaves 2-6,
40 inches, dark dull green.
Leaflets 40-60, 10 x 0.75
inch, 2 secondary ribs on
underside, terminal leaf-
let small. Flowerstalk
20 inches, yellow green.
Fruit 0.25 inch.

Among the many other Chamaedoreas that may be here
are C. klotzchiana, a single trunked species with wide
leaflets in groups along the stem, and C. sartorii, also
solitary, much like C. oblongata, with narrower (2 inches) and less contorted leaflets.

REINHARDTIA

The smallest known palms belong to this genus. At this time, 8 species are recognized, and one of them has four varieties. They are of Central American origin. Although most often encountered as potted plants, they can and do grow out of doors in South Florida. They require deep shade, rich soil, and ample moisture. One species is now sparingly available.

REINHARDTIA GRACILIS

The multiple stems are only 1/4 inch thick, and the palm less than 4 feet high. The stems are brown, the ring-scars gray. There is no true crownshaft, although several dead leafstem bases partly encircle the trunk and hang on after the fall of the leaf.

The leafstem is very short. The leaves are the same medium green on both sides. The leaflets are, for the most part, undivided, forming 2, or more rarely 3 or 4, groups along each side of the leafstem. At the base of adjoining leaflets there may be a "window." The margins are not ribbed, and the leaflet tips are jagged.

The flower stalks appear within the leafy crown, the slender stalks possessing several branches. One female flower grows between two males.

The varieties of R. gracilis are gracilis, gracilior, rostrata, and tenuissima. They differ in the number of ribs on each side of the leafstem. Gracilis has 14 to 22, gracilior has 8 to 11, rostrata has 11 to 15, and tenuissima has 8 to 9. Another difference is in the number of stamens in each flower. Gracilis and tenuissima have 16 to 22, the others 8 to 10.

to 40 inches x 0.25 inch
3-20 leaves 10 inches long
stems 3 inches
16-44 midribs 4 inches long
flowerstalk 6 inches
fruit 0.1 inch, green

ALLAGOPTERA

Brazil, the home of so many of South Florida's newly acquired palms, has given us the Allagoptera. It is the only one in its genus. It is a seashore palm, and grows in the sand dunes just above the tide. It should do excellently in this part of the state. Specimens grown in the shade contrast poorly with those planted in full sunlight.

ALLAGOPTERA ARENARIA
The palm is completely trunkless. Several clusters of leaves and flower stalks arise from the same seed, so the species must be considered to be multiple.

The leaves are a dark green above and silvery below. The leaflets are spaced irregularly along the leafstem, usually in groups of three, and are tough, narrow, and sharply pointed. In each group of 3 leaflets, one will be parallel to the leafstem, another at 45 degrees to it, and the third at 90 degrees, often touching the leaflet from the other side of the leaf.

The flower stalk is surmounted by a very long, thin, narrow, woody spathe. The stalk itself is unbranched. Flowers, of both sexes, are clustered at the tip of the stalk. The top shaped fruit is crowded to the point of one compressing another.

3-5 feet , no trunk
16-20 leaves 40 inches
stems 10-16 inches
40 leaflets 10 x 0.75 inch
flowerstalk 20 inches
fruit 0.5 inch
green and yellow

215

PALMS NOT RECOMMENDED

Some palms are not at home in our climate. Anyone wishing to grow them must make special provisions to duplicate, as nearly as possible, the climatic features of the palm's homeland. This can mean conservatory care, with light, heat, and water carefully regulated, calling for an outlay of time and money beyond the means of the average homeowner.

Among those that are too tender for ordinary garden use are the Lipstick Palms (Cyrtostachys), Astrogyne martiana, Areca triandra and langloisiana, the Mauritias, and Phoenicophorum. Many other species might be appended here, but most are still completely unknown to the public, and it would serve little purpose to list them.

There are palms that prefer a cooler climate than that of South Florida. The Chilean Wine Palm, Jubaea chilensis, and the Windmill Palms, Trachycarpus, are among this number.

Palms of the Mexican deserts, such as the Braheas, can survive here, but many individuals fail to reach maturity. The Nipa Palm, of tropical Asia, does not find the right degree of salinity along our shorelines.

It must be obvious that the palms which adapt best to our climate are those that grow in regions that are similar to our own, in soils, weather, and water conditions. It is remarkable, not that so many palms will not grow here, but that so many will.

LIST OF ADDITIONAL PALMS

The following species have been grown in South Florida, and can be recommended. Obtaining them may be another matter, as they are not common with us, and few, if any, nurseries stock them now.

PALMATE SPECIES

COCCOTHRINAX FRAGRANS -- Cuba. Trunk to 20 feet x 4 inches, smooth; wide segments dark, shiny above, dull gray beneath, moderately lax, twisted near tip.

COCCOTHRINAX MARTII -- Cuba. Trunk to 28 feet x 10 inches, smooth, tapering; narrow segments stiff, dull green both sides.

COCCOTHRINAX SPISSA -- Hispaniola. Trunk to 26 feet x 12 inches; wide segments dull green and silver above, silvery below, moderately lax.

COLPOTHRINAX WRIGHTII -- Cuba. Trunk to 15 or 25 feet, with globular swelling at maturity. Not spiny.

COPERNICIA ALBA -- Cuba. Resembles C. prunifera, but leafstem bases 2 inches wide, leaf segments more lax. Tubular spathes on each flowerstalk branch.

COPERNICIA BERTROANA -- Hispaniola. Trunk ringed, 13 to 17 feet; leaves 3 1/2 feet wide on stems 3 feet; young leaves flat, old ones folded. Like C. baileyana.

COPERNICIA FALLAENSE -- Cuba. Trunk 40 to 60 feet, leaves 6 1/2 feet wide, stems 5 1/2 feet. Resembles C. baileyana, but flowers solitary, stalks shorter, stiffer.

COPERNICIA YAREY -- Cuba. Trunk 19 to 28 feet, leaves 4 feet wide, stems 4 feet. Trunk rough with old leafstem bases from ground to crown.

CHELYOCARPUS CHUCO -- Brazil. Trunk 25 feet tall, leaf divided to base along center line.

LICUALA -- Malaysia. Small, shade-dwelling palms, about 12 species now in our area. Names are confused, but all forms seem to do well, and are recommended.

COSTAPALMATE SPECIES

LIVISTONA MARIAE -- Australia. Trunk 2 feet thick, the base swollen; some leafstem bases as thick plates, otherwise clean; crown open; young leaves may be red, soon turn green.

LIVISTONA ROBINSONIANA -- Philippines. Resembles L. australis, but trunk 8 inches wide; a long sheath of light colored fiber and old leaf bases under crown.

LIVISTONA SARIBUS -- Southeast Asia. Leafstems 4 to 8 feet long, segments in groups; teeth 1 inch long and more; sinus stops irregular.

PINNATE SPECIES -- INDUPLICATE

PHOENIX LOUREIRII -- Indo-China. Like P. roebelenii but leaflets in several planes. (Ex-P. humilis.)

PHOENIX PALUDOSA -- India. Resembles P. reclinata, but much smaller, leaflets more flexible.

PHOENIX PUSILLA -- India. Trunks multiple, 1 to 4 feet tall; leaflets in four planes.

PINNATE SPECIES -- REDUPLICATE

ARECA CATECHU -- Malaya. 30-100 feet tall, gray ringed trunk, prominent crownshaft. Leaflets with 2 ribs, jagged tips. Common name, Betel Palm.

LIST OF ADDITIONAL PALMS (continued)

BACTRIS MEXICANA -- Mexico. Resembles B. major, with interrupted leaflets 1 1/4 inch wide, in several planes, each with 3 sets of secondary ribs.

CALYPTROCALYX SPICATUS -- New Guinea. To 40 feet, smooth ringed trunk, no crownshaft. Leaves flat. Flowerstalk, in crown, unbranched.

CALYPTROGYNE GHIESBRECHTIANA -- Central America. Short, often trunkless. Leaflets sickle-shaped.

CALYPTRONOMA DULCIS -- Cuba. Like the coconut, to 30 feet, leaflets arched in cross section. Fruit is under one inch in length.

CHAMBEYRONIA HOOKERI, MACROCARPA -- Australia. Both species to 60 feet tall, large crownshafts. The leaflets 24 to 24 inches x 4 inches; new leaves red.

EUTERPE -- Caribbean through South America. About 40 species; resemble Royals, but only 5-6 inches thick; leaves lax; fruit purple, white, or black, 1/2 to 1 inch.

JUBAEA CHILENSIS -- Chile. 30-80 feet tall x 4-6 feet thick, rough, no crownshaft. Cold hardy (California, French Riviera) but does poorly in South Florida.

MICROCOELUM INSIGNE -- Brazil. Trunk short, thin; leaflets 9 x 1/2 inches, silver on underside. Trunk has no crownshaft.

ONCOSPERMA TIGILLARUM -- Southeast Asia. Multiple trunks. Spines on trunks, leafstem, spathes; leaflets in one plane, tips pointed, 2 ribs on terminal leaflets.

PELAGODOXA HENRYANA -- Marquesas. 20-30 feet, no crownshaft. Leaves undivided, except by wind. Likes moisture, requires extra care.

PTYCHORHAPIS AUGUSTA -- Nicobar Islands. 40-80 feet tall x 8 inches, crownshaft prominent. Leaflets lax, thin, 30 inches long. Fruit scarlet.

PTYCHOSPERMA LATIUS -- Solomon Islands. 20 feet x 4 inches. 18 leaflets 14 x 4 inches, with broad and jagged tips. Crownshaft pale green. Solitary.

PTYCHSPERMA NICOLAI -- Melanesia. Trunks multiple, 9-12 feet x 1 inch. 24 to 28 leaflets 8-12 inches long x 1 inch, set at odd angles to leafstem.

PTYCHOSPERMA PROPINQUUM -- Melanesia. Trunks multiple, 9-12 feet x 1 inch; 18 leaflets 8-9 inches x 2 inches, irregularly spaced, all more or less at same angle to leafstem.

PTYCHOSPERMA -- Melanesia, Australia. Several more Ptychospermas, as yet unnamed, are now grown here.

RAVENEA -- Madagascar. About 10 species, some of them resembling the coconut, with gray leafstems, the midrib raised on the upper side.

SALACCA EDULIS -- Indonesia. Almost trunkless, no crownshaft. Spines on trunk, leafstem, spathe. Leaflets silver beneath, thin, sharp pointed, 2 ribs in last.

SYAGRUS COMOSA -- Brazil. Closely resembles the Queen Palm, Arecastrum romanzoffianum, with wider leaflets, smaller spathes, larger fruit.

SYAGRUS SANCONA -- Brazil. A small tree, ring-scars close set along the trunk 1/2 inch apart, the leafstems smooth.

SYAGRUS WEDDELLIANA -- Brazil. 10 to 12 feet tall, trunk 2 inches thick. Dark brown hair on leafstems.

CALAMUS -- 300 species, Africa through Australia. Climbing is accomplished by long, hooked stems. The leaflets are long and slender. The Rattan Palms.

DAEMONOROPS -- 100 species, Indo-malaysia. Climb by hooks on the extended leafstem tips. Leaflets are long and slender.

DESMONCUS -- About 40 species, tropical America. Climb by hooks on the extended leafstem tips. Leaflets are short and wide.

PALM BOTANY

Species of palms with apparent affinities are placed in a genus. Like genera are placed in higher classes, variously called sub-families, groups, sub-tribes, and tribes. No classification system yet introduced has achieved complete acceptance, and, as continued research discloses new data and as new concepts are formulated, further revisions are inevitable.

In one system (Dr. Harold E. Moore, Jr., 1961) the palm family is divided into nine sub-families. Genera discussed in this book are listed below.

Coryphoideae -- palmate; Acoelorrhaphe, Coccothrinax, Chamaerops, Copernicia, Cryosophila, Licuala, Rhapidophyllum, Rhapis, Schippia, Serenoa, Washingtonia, Zombia; costapalmate, Brahea, Corypha, Livistona, Nannorrhops, Pritchardia, Sabal.

Phoenicoideae -- Phoenix.

Borassoideae -- Bismarckia, Borassus, Hyphaene, Latania.

Caryotoideae --Arenga, Caryota, Wallichia.

Cocoideae -- spiny; Acrocomia, Aiphanes, Astrocaryum, Bactris, Gastrococos: without spines, Allagoptera, Arecastrum, Arikuryroba, Butia, Cocos, Elaeis, Polyandrococos, Syagrus.

Arecoideae -- crownshaft; Archontophoenix, Brassiophoenix, Carpentaria, Chrysalidocarpus, Dictyosperma, Drymophloeus, Hydriastele, Hyophorbe, Ptychosperma, Roystonea, Satakentia, Veitchia: no crownshaft; Chamaedorea, Gaussia, Geonoma, Heterospathe, Howeia, Neodypsis, Opsiandra, Pinanga, Reinhardtia, Synechanthus.

Sub-families not represented in this book are the Lepidocaryoideae, the Phytelephantoideae, and the Nypoideae.

In a later system, (Dr. Moore, 1973) there are 15 groups. Nine of them correspond to the previously established subfamilies, but the old Arecoideae has now been broken down into six new categories, as listed below.

Pseudophoenicoid Palms -- Pseudophoenix

Ceroxyloid Palms -- no genera in this book

Chamaedoroid Palms -- Chamaedorea, Gaussia, Hyophorbe (Mascarena), Opsiandra, Synechanthus

Iriarteoid Palms -- no genera in this book

Podococcoid Palms -- no genera in this book

Arecoid Palms -- Archontophoenix, Brassiophoenix, Carpentaria, Chrysalidocarpus, Dictyosperma, Drymophloeus, Hydriastele, Ptychosperma, Roystonea, Satakentia, Veitchia, Howeia, Neodypsis, Pinanga, Reinhardtia

Geonomoid Palms -- Geonoma

In The Major Groups of Palms
Dr. Moore places the number of palm species at about 2,779, which he divides between 212 genera and 15 major groups.

225

The ability to identify palm species is only a small part of palm study, and those interested in any aspect of palms should know something of palm botany. The following paragraphs touch briefly on some of the less abstruse scientific findings.

Palms are among the plants that possess woody cells, called xylem, that can support the weight of the trunk and the crown, and cells specialized for the transportation of liquids, called phloem. Each kind of cell is linked with others of its kind, forming tissues that are termed fibro-vascular, and placing its possessors in the category of vascular plants, to the exclusion of algae, fungi, mosses, and other lower plants.

Another major dividing line between plant species centers on the development of seeds, an evolutionary advance over the more simple spore. The seed-bearing plants are the gymnosperms and the angiosperms, with the palms being in the latter group. Plants with seeds of two sections are termed dicotyledons, while palms, with many other plants, have all of the seed tissue in one unit, and are called monocotyledons.

In classifying palm species, attention is paid to the appearance of the trunk, to the design and peculiarities of the leaf, to the structure of the flowerstalk, and, as most significant, the details of the flowers. Botanists are generally agreed that floral structures evolve more slowly than other plant features, and offer more proof of relationships to other plants and plant groups.

Most hardwood trees have a specialized protective layer of dead cells, the outer bark, overlying living cambium tissue. As the tree grows, the cambium cells add to the thickness of the trunk. The interior cellular mass is technically dead, though it functions as a liquid transference medium.

Palm trees have no cambium layer and no true bark. The interior of the trunk is vascular bundles, dead cells that provide support and transport liquids. The exterior is of the same composition, different only in alteration by the elements.

Palms do not increase in width by adding layers outward from the center, although some of them may bulge a bit due to the expansion of water storage cells. Palms achieve the width of the trunk of the mature tree while very young, often with the trunk still below the ground.

Palm trunks can be straight and tall, curving, rambling along the ground, or twisting beneath it. Thickness varies from a fraction of an inch to over three feet. Most trunks are solitary, but many are multiple because of branching at ground level, or because of propagation by underground runners. A very few branch above the ground. Trunks may be smooth, ringed, hairy, rough, or covered with leafbases, rootspines, or sharp needles.

The summit of the trunk is the bud. This is the growth center of the upper end of the trunk. Another such center exists at the heart of the root system. The bud appears as an undifferentiated lump of cells, overlaid with a series of hoods, each one larger than the one below it, and each one an embryo leaf.

Palm leaves begin as a separation of the top layer of the bud. One leaf separates at a time, growing in complexity as others are started below it, until the one next below it pushes through it. The development of each leaf is most pronounced in one direction from the center of the tree, and it is in that direction that the leaf grows and, eventually, radiates outward from the trunk. Each leaf, then, begins as a cover of the bud, then becomes a sheath around it. In some palms, the base of the leaf continues to surround the bud and the newly developed leaves until it matures and finally falls; in other species, the leafbase draws to the side, and in the mature leaf no sheath exists.

Palm leaves are essentially alternate, in that only one is generated at a time. This is true even of the few palms that produce leaves only in one axis, on opposing sides (Wallichia, as an example).

In a few palm species, the leaf has no stem. Where the stem is present, it may be clean and smooth on both upper and lower surface, or, with some species, the lower surface may be studded with randomly placed needles. The margins are without teeth, in most of the species, but a considerable number have sharp triangular teeth. Others have jagged plates, or fibers that can be soft and flexible or hard and sharp pointed, or modified leaflets that have become blunt projections or sharp and spiny.

In the palms with palmate or costapalmate leaves, the leafstem usually terminates in a thin, flat or curved, plate, called a hastula, just above the confluence of the segments. In a few species, a second hastula occurs on the underside of the leaf.

Within each palm species, the number of leaves on the mature adults tend to be within a narrow range. As an old leaf dies and falls, a new one is developing within the crown, and each surviving leaf achieves a lower position relative to the bud, which is increasing its distance from the base of the tree.

The major leaf types (palmate, costapalmate, and pinnate) have been dealt with in the fore part of this book. It might be mentioned, however, that the fishtail leaflet leaf is considered to be pinnate. Induplication and reduplication have also been explained, but it should be noted that the segments of palmate and costapalmate leaves are induplicate.

Segments and leaflets are supported by interior ribs. In most cases, the central rib is greatly enlarged. The marginal ribs, and internal ribs of secondary importance, may be noticeable; finer lines, usually called veins, are always present. In some of the pinnate species, the terminal leaflet is comprised of several undivided leaflets, each one identifiable by its rib. Segments and leaflets, in most species, have smooth margins, but some have teeth, and others have spiny projections where veins have intersected the edge. Tips of segments and leaflets are sharp pointed, in all but a few palm species, although there may be enough die-back to cause the tip to appear to be truncated. In other species, the tip will split; in a few, it is divided, and in one (Carpentaria) it is four-pronged. With species such as the Ptychospermas, the tip appears to have had the end trimmed jaggedly.

The spiny palms all have needles on the leafstem, and may have the same armament on the flowerstalk envelope, on the trunk, and even on the midrib of each leaflet. A few species have random spines on the leaflet margins.

Palm species have little agreement on matters sexual. In some species, each flower has both male and female organs. In others, a portion of the flowers will combine the sexes, and the rest of the flowers will be all males. Many palms have the flowers of both sexes separately, usually with the more numerous males either grouped around the famale (usually three to one), or in a line with the female at the end, or at the tips of the flowerstalk branchlets while the females are at the basal end. In any case, the males mature and fall before the female flowers open, thus guarding against self-pollination. Only a few palms go all the way in the separation of the sexes, with some trees bearing only male flowers and the others only the females.

Palm species have several modes of flowering. One of the least common is typical of the Coryphas, wherein a spire shoots upward from the crown, developes branches and branchlets, and then sets vast quantities of flowers. When these have matured into fruit and have fallen, the tree dies. Another style, equally drastic, is the one followed by the Caryotas, that signal their maturity by the production of a flowerstalk at the top of the tree, then others at each successive node down to the ground. Again, when the fruit ripens, the trunk of the tree dies. Multiple trunked Caryotas replace the deceased tree with a new one, but no such happening occurs in the case of the solitary trunked species.

Crownshaft palms grow the flowerstalks just below the crown, though in actuality the flowerstalks begin their development while wrapped within the clasping leafstem base, but become apparent only when the leaf falls. Palms other than crownshaft palms carry the flowerstalk among the leaves, generally one flowerstalk from any one leaf axil, though not every leaf produces a flowerstalk. A very few palms, such as Opsiandra, have the flowerstalks at intervals on the trunk. Those palms that lack the trunk must send up a flowerstalk from the ground. With all of these species, flowering is continued over a period of years.

Palm flowers exhibit considerable variability from the basic pattern, which is that of a cup (calyx) of three modified leaves (sepals) surrounding the three petals, inside of which there are six filaments and the pollen-bearing anthers, grouped around the three parted female structures. However, there can be only two sepals, or sometimes more than three, and they can be distinctly separate, overlapping, nearly joined, or united. The petals may be missing entirely, or may be present and separate or combined into one unit. The anthers and filaments, the male portion of the flower, may be as few as three, or may number almost 300, but six is usual. The anthers are of different shapes, but it takes magnification to make them available for study. The same may be said for the female organs, the styles, carpels, and the ovules.

Each palm fruit has one seed: in the few exceptions to this rule, there may be two, three, or ten seeds. The largest fruit in the plant kingdom is that of the Double Coconut, or Coco-de-Mer (Lodoicea maldivica), weighing up to 50 pounds, over a foot in length, and so dense that it will not float. One of the smallest must be that of the Reinhardtias, about one-tenth of an inch long.

The exterior of the palm fruit is usually smooth, but some are hairy, others scaly. The remains of the floral parts can be at the top of the fruit, at the side, or near the base. Under the skin, the fruit may be a mass of fibers, or a succulent (though not always edible) flesh, or completely dry. Seeds of the various species differ internally, but this is another matter that is too technical for this book.

Botanists are continually changing plant names, to
the dismay of the layman. These changes are made
when research indicates that a certain species had been
given a name prior to the time it received the one that
it now bears, or when more careful study discloses
that a species -- or a genus -- was wrongly assigned
a name that has now been found to be inappropriate.

The list below is of some of the name changes that
have been visited upon species mentioned in this book.
The discarded name appears in the left column, and its
replacement in the right.

Acanthorrhiza	Cryosophila
Acanthococos	Acrocomia
Actinophloeus	Ptychosperma
Adonidia merrillii	Veitchia merillii
Aeria	Gaussia
Collinia	Chamaedorea
Cocos plumosa	Arecastrum romanzoffianum
Didymosperma	Arenga and Wallichia
Diplothemium	Allagoptera
Eleutheropetalum	Chamaedorea
Erythea	Brahea
Inodes	Sabal
Kentia belmoreana	Howeia belmoreana
Kentia forsteriana	Howeia forsteriana
Kentia joannis	Veitchia joannis
Kentia macarthurii	Ptychosperma macarthurii
Kentia sanderiana	Ptychosperma sanderianum
Malortiea	Reinhardtia
Martinezia *	Aiphanes
Mascarena	Hyophorbe
Neanthe bella	Chamaedorea elegans
Oreodoxa *	Roystonea
Paurotis	Acoelorrhaphe
Sargentia	Pseudophoenix
Seaforthia	Ptychosperma
Strongylocaryum	Ptychosperma
Tessmanniodoxa	Ptychosperma

The names with asterisks are preferred by some
authorities who do not accept the changes.

PALM GEOGRAPHY

EUROPE
  Chamaerops
AFRICA
  Chamaerops
  Elaeis
  Hyphaene
  Phoenix
INDIAN OCEAN
  Bismarckia
  Chrysalidocarpus
  Dictyosperma
  Hyophorbe
  Latania
  Neodypsis
INDIA
  Arenga
  Borassus

Caryota
Cocos
Corypha
Nannorrhops
Phoenix
Wallichia
MALAYSIA
  Arenga
  Caryota
  Licuala
  Livistona
  Pinanga
  Ptychosperma
CHINA – JAPAN
  Livistona
  Rhapis
  Satakentia
  Trachycarpus

AUSTRALASIA
  Archontophoenix
  Brassiophoenix
  Carpentaria
  Drymophloeus
  Howeia
  Hydriastele
  Livistona
  Ptychosperma
SOUTH SEAS
  Drymophloeus
  Heterospathe
  Pritchardia
  Veitchia
SOUTH AMERICA
  Acrocomia
  Allagoptera

Aiphanes	Aiphanes	Pseudophoenix
Arecastrum	Astrocaryum	Roystonea
Arikuryroba	Chamaedorea	Sabal
Attalea	Coccothrinax	Schippia
Bactris	Cryosophila	Thrinax
Butia	Gastrococos	Zombia
Chamaedorea	Reinhardtia	**U.S. & MEXICO**
Geonoma	Roystonea	Acoelorrhaphe
Jubaea	Synechanthus	Acrocomia
Maximiliana	**CARIBBEAN BASIN**	Brahea
Orbignya	Acoelorrhaphe	Coccothrinax
Roystonea	Acrocomia	Pseudophoenix
Polyandrococos	Aiphanes	Rhapidophyllum
Scheelea	Copernicia	Roystonea
Syagrus	Gaussia	Sabal
CENTRAL AMERICA	Geonoma	Serenoa
Acoelorrhaphe	Opsiandra	Thrinax
Acrocomia		Washingtonia 233

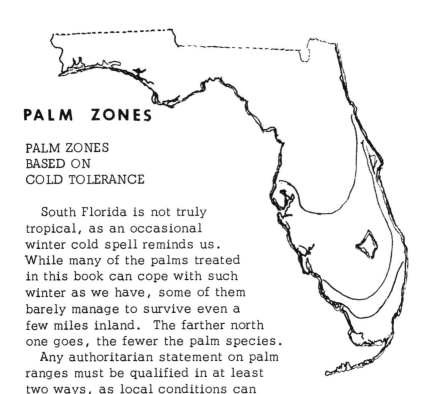

PALM ZONES

PALM ZONES
BASED ON
COLD TOLERANCE

    South Florida is not truly
tropical, as an occasional
winter cold spell reminds us.
While many of the palms treated
in this book can cope with such
winter as we have, some of them
barely manage to survive even a
few miles inland. The farther north
one goes, the fewer the palm species.

    Any authoritarian statement on palm
ranges must be qualified in at least
two ways, as local conditions can
always be found to contradict a general rule, and no
one can claim complete personal experience with all
the many species under all circumstances. The data
offered here is conservative, in the sense that to rely
on it should prevent a palm fancier from investing in
palms that cannot be expected to adapt to his region,
but it may keep him from experimenting and finding
that some species not recommended might make it.

PALMS FOR EXTREME SOUTH FLORIDA -- ZONE 1

Allagoptera	Carpentaria	Pinanga
Aiphanes	Cocos	Polyandrococos
Archontophoenix	Corypha	Reinhardtia
Arenga	Gaussia	Satakentia
Arikuryroba	Geonoma	S. Amer. Oil Palms
Bactris	Heterospathe	Synechanthus
Brassiophoenix	Hydriastele	Veitchia
	Opsiandra	

PALMS FOR EAST COAST AND SOUTH FLORIDA -- ZONE 1,2

Acrocomia	Elaeis	Licuala
Caryota	Gastrococos	Neodypsis
Chamaedorea	Copernicia	Pritchardia
Chrysalidocarpus	Howeia	Ptychosperma
Cryosophila	Hyophorbe	Schippia
Dictyosperma	Hyphaene	Syagrus
Drymophloeus	Latania	Zombia

PALMS FOR CENTRAL AND SOUTH FLORIDA -- ZONE 1,2,3

Acoelorrhaphe	Coccothrinax	Rhapis
Arecastrum	Erythea	Roystonea
Bismarckia	Livistona	Washingtonia
Borassus	Phoenix	

PALMS FOR ALL FLORIDA REGIONS -- ZONES 1,2,3,4

Butia	Nannorrhops	Sabal
Chamaerops	Rhapidophyllum	Serenoa

PALMS FOR NORTH FLORIDA ONLY

Jubaea	Trachycarpus

Seedling palms are always far more tender than well established adults. A palm that is in good health, with plenty of water in the ground around it, can be expected to live through a cold spell that kills a sickly member of the same species growing beside it.

Nothing can take the place of local experience with palms. Lists such as this one should be disregarded when they are in conflict with observations of people actively engaged in growing palms in the neighborhood where one lives.

PALM CARE

Readers interested in the proper care of palms are advised to read Cultivated Palms, a special issue of the American Horticultural Magazine, January, 1961. Although it has been out of print for years, it is one of the best sources for information on propagation, fertilizing, pruning, insects, diseases, cold tolerance, and special garden uses, among other topics. The two articles that follow are from data in that book, as is the information given below, given here in the case that the book may not be obtainable.

An all purpose fertilizer is generally recommended for palms, 6-6-6 or 9-6-6 (nitrogen, phosphoric acid, potash), with 6-6-6-3 (the last is magnesium) for South Florida. Two applications (late winter and mid-summer) is best for palms in the northern half of the state, while a third application should be given those palms in the southern half. Very small palms can be given as little as one to two ounces of fertilizer, while large, mature specimens need about fifteen pounds. Where obtainable, organic fertilizer is preferable. As examples, cottonseed meal, ground steamed bone meal, tankage, blood, guano, fish scraps, and manures are all highly recommended.

Deficiencies in certain chemicals are manifested in the poor appearance of the palm. The lack of nitrogen, potash, manganese, copper, magnesium, boron, zinc, sulphur, molybdenum, or iron can adversely affect the health of the tree.

Questions on selection, care, and diseases of palms can be best answered by the local County Cooperative Extension Department. This organization is an amalgam of federal and state plant services. Its officials have the training and experience to advise the homeowner on all plant problems, and they are aware of the latest and best procedures in palm care.

Palms are subject to many diseases, some restricted to one species or to one genus, others less selective. Various fungi may attack wet leaves, causing spotting (areas of damaged tissue) that may spread until the entire leaf is dead. Other fungi, and some bacteria, have been blamed for a rotting of the bud, especially in the Coconut Palm.

One of the worst palm diseases is infestation by the fungus Ganoderma sulcatum. The spores are thought to enter the tissues of the tree through wounds, from whence they spread through the base of the tree. The lower leaves die off, and the new leaves are stunted. Then the fruiting body of the fungus appears on the outside of the trunk, just above the ground. Infected trees should be removed and burned, as there is no cure at the present time.

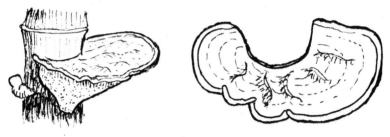

Lethal yellowing is now (1973) thought to be a mycoplasm, a primitive form of fungus. Coconut palms that have become host to the parasite loose the fruit, after which the leaves, starting with the lower ones, turn yellow and fall. The disease has been suspected in the deaths of Veitchias, Pritchardias, Arikuryrobas, and Washingtonias -- and this list is probably incomplete. No permanent cure is known, but experimental work with terramycin offers some hope.

Seedling palms are vulnerable to the attack of mites, thrips, aphids, and scale insects. Mites eat the top layer of leaf cells; a serious infestation of mites can be fatal to the seedling, unless controlled. The others suck plant juices, and may slow the growth of the plant but will seldom kill it. Thread scale, appearing as a hard, black thread that slowly lengthens, is especially hard to combat.

Ambrosia beetles, one-tenth of an inch long, bore pencil-lead size holes in tree trunks and introduce a fungus on which the larvae feed. Healthy trees flush the borings with sap flow, while trees of low vitality may succomb to the combination of troubles.

The palmetto weevil, Rhynchophorus, is a serious pest of the Canary Island Date, the Coconut, and the Latan Palms. The eggs are laid in the bud, and the larvae (the edible "gru-gru" of Puerto Rico) consume the base of the young leaves, sometimes burrowing through the trunk to the roots. When new leaves fall over, their bases undermined, the presence of the palmetto weevil should be suspected. Drenching the bud with insecticide often saves the tree.

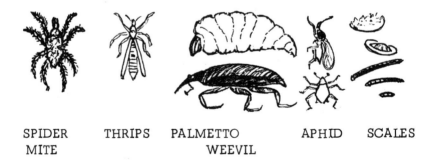

SPIDER   THRIPS   PALMETTO   APHID   SCALES
MITE   WEEVIL

SALT TOLERANCE

Most palms have a high degree of tolerance for salt, and more experimentation may well disclose that many species thought to be tender in this regard can thrive along the coast, within a few yards of the sea.

The following genera can be trusted to flourish where exposure to sea winds is constant.

Allagoptera	Cocos	Sabal
Butia	Mascarena	Serenoa
Chamaerops	Pritchardia	Thrinax
Coccothrinax	Pseudophoenix	Trachycarpus

Members of the following genera have been drenched by hurricane tides, in some cases the crown submerged, and have shown no ill effects. Very possibly, some of them could do well at the shore line, but evidence for this is lacking.

Acoelorrhaphe	Copernicia	Phoenix
Acrocomia	Corypha	Ptychosperma
Aiphanes	Cryosophila	Rhapis
Arecastrum	Dictyosperma	Roystonea
Arenga	Elaeis	Schippia
Arikuryroba	Erythea	S. Amer. Oil
Bactris	Hyphaene	Syagrus
Bismarckia	Latania	Veitchia
Borassus	Licuala	Wallichia
Caryota	Livistona	Washingtonia
Chrysalidocarpus	Nannorrhops	Zombia

The test the above palms passed was not given to the following. They might do as well, however.

Brassiophoenix	Heterospathe	Pinanga
Drymophloeus	Howeia	Polyandrococos
Gastrococos	Hydriastele	Reinhardtia
Gaussia	Opsiandra	Rhapidophyllum

Chamaedorea and Geonoma species have been killed by drenching in salt water of several hours duration.

PALMS FOR CONTAINERS

Palms of certain species make good container plants. Of the species discussed in this book, the following can be recommended.

Chamaedorea (any)   Licuala grandis
Chamaerops humilis   Licuala spinosa
Chrysalidocarpus lutescens   Phoenix roebelenii
Coccothrinax argentata   Pinanga kuhlii
Drymophloeus beguinii   Reinhardtia gracilis
Howeia belmoreana   Rhapis excelsa
Howeia forsteriana   Rhapis humilis

Some larger species can be used effectively as pot plants when small, but must be expected to grow to an unmanageable size for an indoor species. These would include those below.

Aiphanes caryotafolia   Livistona rotundifolia
Archontophoenix (both)   Paurotis wrightii
Arecastrum romanzoffianum   Phoenix canariensis
Butia capitata   Phoenix reclinata
Caryota mitis   Phoenix rupicola
Caryota urens   Ptychosperma elegans
Cocos nucifera   Ptychosperma macarthurii
Dictyosperma album   Thrinax floridana
Heterospathe elata   Veitchia merrillii
Livistona chinensis   Washingtonia robusta

Again, the book Cultivated Palms has excellent advice on the care of potted palms. The most critical factor is the watering of them. Two or three waterings a week are recommended, with sufficient water given each time so that some of it drains through the pot and out through the bottom. Soils for potted plants should be light and porous, or even sandy. Humus, leaf mold, or peat may be mixed with it. Balanced, inorganic and organic, fertilizers should be used. In cold climates, the use of fertilizer should be curtailed during the winter.

PRONUNCIATION GUIDE

     Botanical Latin is a written language, and has no
accepted rules of pronunciation. In constructing this
guide, I have tried to set down syllables and accents
as they are used by people whose judgement and
experience I respect.

Aceolorrhaphe (ah-see-lo-RAY-fee) wrightii (RITE-ee-eye)
Acrocomia (ak-kro-COE-mee-ah) aculeata (ah-kyu-lee-
    AH-tah) totai (TOE-tie)
Aiphanes (ah-IF-ah-nees) acanthophylla (ah-can-tho-FILL-
    ah) caryotaefolia (car-ee-yoe-tee-FOE-lee-ah)
Allagoptera (al-lah-GOP-ter-ah) arenaria (ah-ren-NARE-
    ee-yah)
Archontophoenix (ark-on-toe-FEE-niks) alexandrae (ahl-eks-
    ANN-dree) cunninghamiana (cun-ing-ham-ee-ANN-ah)
Arecastrum (as-ree-CAS-trum) romanzoffianum (rome-an-
    zoff-ee-ANN-um)
Arenga (ah-RENG-ah) engleri (ENG-ler-eye) microcarpa
    (my-kro-KAR-pah) pinnata (pin-NAH-tah) tremula
    (TREM-you-lah)
Arikuryroba (ah-rih-coo-ree-ROW-bah) schizophylla (skitz-
    oh-FILL-ah)
Astrocaryum (as-troh-CAR-yum) mexicanum (mex-eh-CAN-um)
Attalea (at-tah-LEE-ah)
Bactris (BAK-tris) gasipaes (GAS-ih-paze) major (MAY-jore)
Bismarckia (biz-MARK-ee-ah) nobilis (no-BILL-is)
Borassus (bo-RASS-us) flabellifer (flah-BELL-ih-fer)
Brahea (BRAY-hee-ah) armata (are-MAH-tah)
Brassiophoenix (bras-ee-oh-FEE-niks)
Butia (BUE-tee-ah) capitata (cap-ih-TAH-tah)
Carpentaria (car-pen-TARE-ee-ah) acuminata (ak-cue-min-
    AH-tah)
Caryota (car-ree-OH-tah) cumingii (coo-MING-ee-eye)
    mitis (MY-tis) urens (YOU-rens)
Chamaedorea (kam-ee-DORE-ee-ah) arenbergiana (Ah-ren-
    berg-ee-AH-nah) cataractarum (cat-ah-rack-TARE-um)
    concolor (kon-CULL-or) elatior (ee-LAH-tee-or)
    ernesti-angusti (ur-NESS-tee aw-GUSS-tee) erumpens
    (ee-RUM-pens) glaucifolia (glows-sih-FOLE-ee-ah)

metallica (met-TAL-ih-kah) microspadix (my-kro-SPAY-dicks) oblongata (ob-lon-GAH-tah) radicalis (rad-ih-CAL-is) seifrizii (see-FRITZ-ee-eye) tepejilote (tay-pay-hee-LOE-tay)

Chamaerops (KAM-ee-rops) humilis (HUE-mil-is)

Chrysalidocarpus (CRY-sal-id-oh-CAR-pus) cabadae (kah-BAH-dee) lucubensis (loo-cue-BEN-sis) lutescens (loo-TESS-sens)

Coccothrinax (cock-oh-THRY-naks) argentata (ar-gen-TAH-tah) argentea (ar-GEN-tee-ah) crinita (krin-EE-tah) dussiana (duss-ee-AH-nah) miraguama (meer-ah-GWAM-mah)

Cocos (KOH-kos) nucifera (new-SIF-er-ah)

Copernicia (koe-per-NEE-see-ah) baileyana (bay-lee-ANN-ah) glabrescens (glab-RES-sens) macroglossa (mack-roe-GLOSS-ah) prunifera (prue-NIF-er-ah) rigida (RID-jid-dah)

Corypha (coe-RYE-fah) elata (ee-LAH-tah) umbraculifera (um-brak-you-LIFF-er-ah)

Cryosophila (cry-oh-SOF-ih-lah) argentea (ar-GEN-tee-ah) warscewiczii (war-see-WITZ-ee-eye)

Dictyosperma (dik-tee-oh-SPER-mah) album (ALL-bum) aureum (AWE-ree-um)

Drymophloeus (dry-moe-FLEE-us) beguinii (bee-GWEEN-ee-eye) olivaeformis (aw-liv-eye-FORM-is)

Elaeis (ee-LAY-iss) guineensis (ginn-ee-EN-sis)

Gastrococos (gas-troh-COE-kos) crispa (KRIS-pah)

Gaussia (GOWSS-ee-ah) attenuata (ah-ten-you-AH-tah) princeps (PRIN-seps)

Geonoma (jee-oh-NO-mah) interrupta (in-ter-RUP-tah)

Heterospathe (het-er-oh-SPAY-thee) elata (ee-LAH-tah)

Howeia (HOW-ee-ah) belmoreana (bel-more-ee-AH-nah) forsteriana (for-stir-ee-ANN-ah)

Hydriastele (HID-ree-ah-STEE-lee)

Hyphaene (high-FEE-nee)

Hyophorbe (high-FORE-bee) revaughnii (re-VONN-ee-eye) Lagenacaulis (lah-jee-nih-CAUL-is) verschaffeltii (vers-shah-FELL-tee-eye)

Latania (la-TANE-ee-ah) loddegesii (loh-dih-GEEZ-ee-eye) lontaroides (lon-tah-ROY-dees) verschaffeltii (vers-shah-FELL-tee-eye)

Licuala (lick-you-AH-lah) grandis (GRAND-iss)

Livistona (liv-iss-TONE-ah) australis (os-TRAL-iss) chinensis (chey-NEN-sis) decipiens (dee-SIP-ee-ens) rotundifolia (roe-tun-dih-FOE-lee-ah)

Maximiliana (macks÷i- mill-ee-ANN-ah)

Nannorrhops (NAN-or-rops) ritchiana (rit-chee-ANN-ah)

Neodypsis (nee-oh-DIP-sis) decaryi (dee-CAR-yee)

Opsiandra (op-see-ANN-dra) maya (MY-ah)

Orbignya (or-BIG-nee-ah)

Phoenix (FEE-niks) canariensis (can-ay-ree-EN-sis) dactylifera (dak-till-IF-er-ah) reclinata (rek-lin-AH-tah) roebelenii (reb-bel-EN-ee-eye) rupicola (roo-PIK-oh-lah) sylvestris (sil-VES-tris)

Pinanga (pin-NANG-ah) kuhlii (COOL-ee-eye)

Polyandrococos (poll-ee-an-dro-COE-cos) caudescens (caw-DESS-sens)

Pritchardia (prit-CHARD-ee-ah) pacifica (pah-SIF-ih-kah) thurstonii (THURS-ston-eye)

Pseudophoenix (sue-do-FEE-niks) sargentii (sar-GENT-ee-eye) vinifera (vin-IFF-er-ah)

Ptychosperma (tie-koh-SPER-mah) elegans (ELL-ee-gans) macarthurii (mack-ARE-thur-eye) sanderianum (san-der-ee-ANN-um)

Reinhardtia (rine-HART-ee-ah) gracilis (grah-SILL-is)

Rhapidophyllum (rah-pid-oh-FIE-lum) hystrix (HISS-trix)

Rhapis (RAY-pis) excelsa (ek-SELL-sa)

Roystonea (roy-STONE-ee-ah) borinquena (bore-in-KAY-nah) elata (ee-LAH-tah) oleracea (oh-ler-AY-see-ah) regia (REE-gee-ah)

Sabal (SAY-ball) causiarum (cows-ee-ARE-um) etonia (eh-toe-NIGH-ah) mauritiiformis (more-it-ee-eye-FORM-is) mexicana (meks-ih-CAN-nah) minor (MY-nor) palmetto (pahl-MET-toe)

Satakentia (sah-tah-KENT-ee-ah) liukiuensis (lyoo-kyoo-EN-sis)

Scheelea (SHEE-lee-ah)

Schippia (SHIP-ee-ah) concolor (con-CULL-or)

Serenoa (sair-ee-NOE-ah) repens (REP-ens)

Syagrus (sigh-AG-russ) coronata (co-ro-NAH-tah)

Synechanthus (sin-ee-CHAN-thus) fibrosus (fie-BRO-sus)

Trachycarpus (tray-kee-CAR-pus) fortunei (FOR-chune-eye)

Thrinax (THRY-nacks) excelsa (ek-SELL-sah) floridana (flor-ih-DAN-ah) microcarpa (my-cro-CAR-pah)

Wallichia (wall-ICK-ee-ah) disticha (DISS-tik-ah)

Washingtonia (wash-ing-TONE-ee-ah) filifera (fill-IF-er-ah) robusta (roe-BUSS-tah)

Veitchia (VAYTCH-ee-ah) arecina (are-ee-SEE-nah) joannis (jo-ANN-iss) macdanielsii (mack-DAN-yels-eye) merrillii (MARE-ill-eye) montgomeryana (mont-gom-er-ee-ANN-ah) winin (WIN-in)

Zombia (ZOM-bee-ah) antillarum (an-till-ARE-um)

NOTES

INDEX OF COMMON NAMES

Many palms are known to us by the generic name (as Washingtonia, Licuala, etc.) rather than by an English or a native name.

INDEX

Entries marked with an asterisk have not been given full treatment in the text. Either they are so rare as to be practically unobtainable here, or they have failed to prove themselves under average growing conditions, and cannot be recommended.